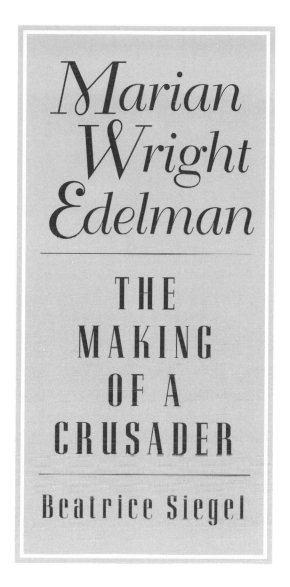

Marian Wright Edelman

THE MAKING OF A CRUSADER

Beatrice Siegel

SIMON & SCHUSTER BOOKS FOR YOUNG READERS

SIMON & SCHUSTER BOOKS FOR YOUNG READERS
An imprint of Simon & Schuster Children's Publishing Division
1230 Avenue of the Americas
New York, New York 10020

Designed by Christy Hale
The text of this book is set in Electra.
Manufactured in the United States of America
10 9 8 7 6 5 4 3 2 1

Special thanks to Harold Ober Associates Incorporated, for permission to reprint
"Tell Me" by Langston Hughes, copyright © 1951 by Langston Hughes.
Copyright renewed 1979 by George Houston Bass.
Also thanks to Beacon Press, for permission to reprint "O God Of All Children,"
from *Guide My Feet: Meditations and Prayers on Loving, Living
With and Working for Children* by Marian Wright Edelman, copyright ©
1995 by Marian Wright Edelman.

Page 147 constitutes an extension of the copyright page.

Library of Congress Cataloging-in-Publication Data

Siegel, Beatrice.
Marian Wright Edelman : the making of a crusader / Beatrice Siegel.
p. cm.
Includes bibliographical references and index.
ISBN 0-02-782629-5
1. Edelman, Marian Wright—Juvenile literature. 2. Afro-Americans—Biography—Juvenile literature.
3. Social reformers—United States—Biography—Juvenile literature. 4. Children's rights—United States—
History—20th century—Juvenile literature. 5. Civil rights workers—United States—Biography—Juvenile
literature. [1. Edelman, Marian Wright. 2. Afro-Americans—Biography. 3. Women—biography.
4. Reformers. 5. Children's rights.] I. Title.
E185.97.E33S54 1995 362.7'092—dc20 [B] 94-41245

For my husband Sam

CONTENTS

Tell Me

Why should it be *my* loneliness,
Why should it be *my* song,
Why should it be *my* dream,
      deferred
      overlong?

—LANGSTON HUGHES

CHAPTER ONE

A Call to Action

FIFTEEN HUNDRED PEOPLE STOOD UP AND APPLAUDED the keynote speaker. She was there to address the luncheon audience of the National Black Child Development Institute at the New York Hilton and Tower Hotel in October 1993. Greeting the assembled guests with a warm smile, she started her talk. Her subject? Children of the United States and African-American children in particular.

Her opening statement startled the audience: "We have come a long way in the African-American community," she said, but we now face "the worst crisis since slavery."

The speaker—Marian Wright Edelman—is known by millions across the country as a crusader on behalf of children. She is passionately committed to their care and survival, and on their behalf she tugs at the conscience of her listeners and arouses them to action.

Expanding on the latest catastrophes, she conveyed the bleak reality for too many children today: violence, guns, drugs, and teenage pregnancy. In many African-American communities, she said, two-thirds of all black families with children are female-headed households; thousands of children live in foster care or are taken care of by grandparents; there is a widening gap between black and white infant deaths. In these communities, she said, "infants are more likely to die than babies in Cuba, Bulgaria, and Kuwait, and we must ask ourselves why we are standing for that."

"Though the threat of lynching no longer hangs over our people," she continued, "death by guns and preventable sickness and poverty remain a daily reality." She cited the chilling figures, "an American child is murdered in this country every two hours. Twenty-five children, the equivalent of a classroom full, are murdered by guns in this country every three days."

"Get the guns off the streets!" she demanded. "Stand up and say to those who kill our children, and to children who are killing children, that this is not something we are going to stand for."

Her words now blunt and impassioned, she spoke about AIDS and about "prisons bulging with our young men," men who see prison as a better alternative to the streets and premature death. She added to the wanton killing and neglect the "plague of drugs"—the sexually transmitted diseases, and the cultural messages that glamorize sex, alcohol, tobacco, and violence.

Show that you care! Let children know that you are there to fight with them and for them; that you are there to help them fight the hardships and the terrors, she urged. Open your homes and your churches; open your hearts and help rebuild the safety and natural support children once had.

Waves of applause greeted her appeal that people get involved, that they help change conditions. She asked her audience to make the nineties the decade for children; to build a massive and sustained crusade that would leave no child behind.

Sounding a more encouraging note, she described the project of a group of black college students who are now working with children and opening Freedom schools in urban centers. Often these students become the caring adults children need.

She also reminded the audience about new funds for poor families made available by the Clinton administration. She appealed to parents and teachers to see to it that every child is immunized against childhood diseases and that Head Start programs are expanded and updated.

Develop a strategy, a voice; develop a vision, she insisted in a forceful conclusion. See that each and every child is provided for; that we build a more just society.

"All children belong to us," she said.

She ended her talk with a prayer she had written called "O God Of All Children." By the end of the last lines there were few dry eyes in the audience.

> O God of children of destiny and of despair,
>
>   of war and of peace,
>
> Of disfigured, diseased, and dying children,
>
> Of children without hope and of children with hope
>
>   to spare and to share,
>
> *Help us to love and respect and protect them all.*

CHAPTER TWO

Childhood

MARIAN WRIGHT WAS BORN AND LIVED HER YOUNG years in Bennettsville, in the northeast corner of South Carolina. The town often seemed fixed in time, especially in the 1940s and 1950s. In those years, it was an agricultural center for the huge farms growing cotton, tobacco, and grains across the flat, fertile, wide open spaces. Its seat as the capital of Marlboro County gave the town distinction, bringing to the broad avenues a show of large law offices, the courthouse, schools, and a public library.

It was a small town. Only 7,005 people lived in Bennettsville according to the 1940 census. The whole county that year had some 33,000 residents.

It was also a town with a long history. Stout tall trees told its age in the knotted roots that broke through the sidewalks and in the long, broad branches of tangled foliage. The stately homes on Main Street sat far back on carefully tended lawns bordered with flowering shrubs. In the spring and summer, the neighborhoods were vivid with the bright colors of lavender wisteria, flaming azaleas, pink crape myrtle, and the luxurious creamy blossoms of magnolia trees.

There were children at play whose laughter filled the air and quiet friendly talk in shops and markets. And always there were cheerful greetings along the streets.

Under the soft talk and gracious manner, there was something troubling, uneasy, and uncertain. This was the South, and the small picturesque town was clearly divided into two separate and unequal communities as if a line had been drawn between them. African Americans, who numbered a bit more than half the population, were segregated into the neighborhoods of West Main Street while the white people owned the homes along East Main and everywhere else.

A strong sense of community tied the white residents to one another. They controlled the government, owned the large farms and large homes, and socialized and attended their segregated churches together. A strong sense of community also united the African Americans. They had built the town with their labor, worked the farms, cared for the lawns, and were maids and cooks in the large homes. The African Americans—including a small class of business people and professionals, teachers, and clergy—could not vote or select the town sheriff. They could not participate in political decisions, eat in the town's white restaurants, attend the white clubs, get quality medical care or education, use the public library, drink from the same water fountains, or swim in the town pool. On a hot summer day African-American children could only look across the road at the large swimming pool and know that they could not use it—it was for whites only.

It was a struggle for African Americans to deal with the daily insults and the pervasive and enduring pain of race discrimination, to deal with their rage and their fear.

Within their neighborhoods, families, and churches, they found comfort and safety. Concern for each other created strong bonds of kinship, and the church where they met, prayed, and sang fortified them and gave shape to their hopes and needs.

A strong comforting voice belonged to the Reverend Arthur J. Wright, the pastor of the Shiloh Baptist Church. He was a sensitive man, keenly attuned to the needs of his people. He was also a determined man. Uppermost in his mind was the importance of defining the community and moving it forward so that people could develop their strengths and talents. Racism and segregation were not the topics of weekly sermons. Instead he spoke of the need to transcend these evils, to rise above them

The Wright family. Bottom row: Marian and her friend Ruth.
Back row from left: sister Olive, Mrs. Wright, brother Harry,
the Reverend Wright, and brother Julian

in order to become productive and fulfilled. He insisted that people take responsibility for themselves, and by showing them a way to deal with a racist system, he helped them mute their anger and despair. Everyone, he said, was capable of reaching for the stars.

In the pastor's home was a steel helmet he had worn in World War I. The helmet had a hole in it from a bullet that had grazed his skull and almost killed him. The Reverend Wright's skirmish with death was a turning point in his life. God spared him, he said, and he gave up his job as a letter carrier to devote himself to the ministry. After graduation from the small black Morris College in Sumter, South Carolina, he took

courses at Union Theological Seminary in New York and attended seminars at Oberlin College in Ohio and Hampton Institute in Virginia.

His education never stopped. Tireless, he traveled to other cities to attend lectures, conferences, and meetings. On one occasion, he met the African-American writer and educator Booker T. Washington and was influenced by Washington's advocacy of self-help. "Pull yourselves up by the bootstraps," became the cornerstone of the pastor's teaching.

Perhaps the Reverend Wright also borrowed from the writings of the African-American scholar

The Shiloh Baptist Church in Bennettsville

W. E. B. DuBois, who opposed Booker T. Washington's teachings. DuBois urged blacks not to be subservient but to fight for a place in history, to fight for equal citizenship and equal education and employment.

In the Reverend Wright's leadership there was no accommodation to racism, which he considered evil, nor was there militant resistance to it, but only the necessity to push it aside and move onward.

Essentially, he urged education and self-help in his talks, as he encouraged people to buy land and open small businesses, to develop their own social and economic institutions and their own sense of identity.

The heavenly sounds of music drifting out of the Shiloh Baptist Church revealed the talents of Mrs. Maggie Leola Bowen Wright, married to the pastor and, like him, committed to the community. The daughter of a Baptist minister, she was raised on sermons and church music. To her musical training as a child, she added courses at Oberlin College when she traveled there with Reverend Wright, and she also attended church music seminars during summers. In the year 1929, when the large red-brick church was completed, she became the church organist and choir leader.

Behind a quiet manner was a woman of impressive poise and purposefulness, holding many full-time jobs. In her role of wife and mother, she took care of the home and children. At the same time, she was the church's organist and choir leader. Somehow she also had the energy to found and lead the Mothers Club, to become the chief fund-raiser for the church, and as time went on to undertake other demanding community responsibilities.

Her dignity and directness worked wonders in the surrounding white world. The editor of the local paper would always accede to Mrs. Wright's requests to list notices of church events.

It seemed fitting when the Wrights' fifth and last child was born on

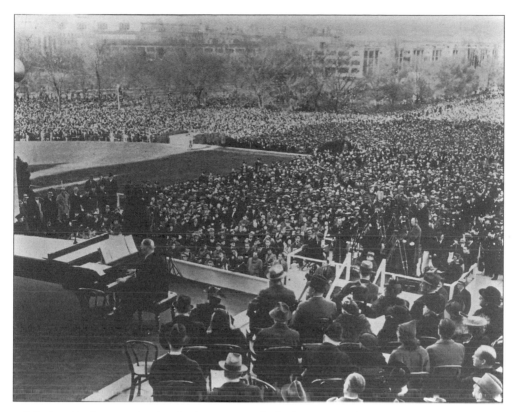
Marian Anderson singing before a crowd of 75,000 people at Lincoln Memorial concert Easter Sunday

June 6, 1939, that they would name her Marian after Marian Anderson. That year, the Daughters of the American Revolution had denied Marian Anderson—the world famous contralto—the right to sing at Constitution Hall in Washington, D.C., because she was African American. The resultant furor expressed the country's outrage. First Lady Eleanor Roosevelt led the protest of the racism by resigning her membership in the DAR and arranging for Ms. Anderson to sing for the public on Easter Sunday on the steps of the Lincoln Memorial. Seventy-five thousand people attended the concert.

As if Marian Anderson did not denote enough fighting spirit, the infant daughter was given the middle name Elizabeth after England's sixteenth-century queen, the fearless and independent Elizabeth I.

The child would benefit from being the youngest in the family. Between her and the oldest child, a sister named Olive, were three brothers: Arthur, Jr.; Harry; and Julian. Separating Marian and the next youngest, Julian, was a seven-year difference. All the siblings were in school, working hard at their studies and working in the church and in the community; and Marian, growing up surrounded by such role models, would soon follow in their footsteps.

CHAPTER THREE

"Assign Yourself"

MARIAN GREW UP IN THE CHURCH PARSONAGE. FOR the first few years it was a white frame house on Cheraw Street. When she was seven the family moved into the newly built, red-brick parsonage. Both homes were spacious, comfortable, and busy. Shelves were filled with her father's library: the volumes of Shakespeare, Carl Sandburg, and W. E. B. DuBois. Magazines came in the mail, among them *Time, Life, Look,* and the *Christian Century.* There were the family car, the new gas stove, the telephone, and the smokehouse full of food. The baby grand piano in the living room meant voice and music lessons.

For a while Mrs. Wright taught Olive and Marian the piano, but then outside teachers were brought in. Eager that her daughters become musicians, Mrs. Wright was delighted at their show of talent. Not only were Olive and Marian musically trained, the sons were also encouraged. Julian played the trumpet and Arthur the clarinet. Between musical instruments and choir practice, the house was filled at all times with the sounds of

The house on Cheraw Street

music: gospel, classical, and popular. The youngest child in the household absorbed the music, and it became a natural part of her life.

Marian's young years were filled with sparkling memories. One was the short-lived family farm. Though her mother thought of the idea, her father saw a farm as a way of teaching his sons a sense of responsibility toward work. They had to milk the 13 cows and care for the chickens and hogs. Marian, tagging along with the older siblings, was often "smacked in the face by cows," she would recall. The reverend also had his sons work during one harvest to instill in them respect for the labor of others.

It was a close-knit family, and it always included the youngest. Marian was never left alone. She joined the family in choir singing, in evenings playing monopoly, and in summer trips to attend seminars at Hampton Institute. She was with her parents when they drove to visit the older children at college or to attend their commencement exercises. And she was with them when they visited sick parishioners.

Mrs. Wright firmly believed the older children had a responsibility toward the youngest. Olive was responsible for combing and braiding Marian's hair, and she could be "rigorous" doing it. Sometimes Marian was not sure she would survive the antics of an older brother gleefully pushing her in a speeding carriage or on "treacherously high swings." In a way she was "pesty," Marian would recall, especially when her older sister, Olive, out walking with a boyfriend, had to keep an eye on her baby sister "tagging along." And Marian would be there poking her head into the motor of a car her brothers were fixing.

Not only did the children interact socially but they were kept busy continuously either working, reading, or studying. Their father was as adamant at home as he was in church about the necessity of people helping each other and educating themselves. For Marian the busy schedule presented no problem. She simply began to read and became another bright Wright child.

Her close childhood friend, Ruth Thomas, would remember that she

Marian, second from right, with scout troop

and Marian read a great deal as youngsters. They took books out of the library at the Marlboro Training High School where they started together in kindergarten and continued through high school. Or Marian's father made books available from his collection. In the evenings, they would discuss the books on the telephone.

At every step of her growth, her father emphasized the importance of education. Often he would pack the family into the car and drive them to hear black speakers lecture in nearby towns. On one occasion they heard poet Langston Hughes, on another former Howard University President Mordecai Johnson. Every evening the hour 6:30 to 7:30 was dedicated to study around the dinner table. Each child had to be busy studying, reading, or pretending to do so. "Assign yourself," the Reverend Wright counseled when one of the children claimed there was no homework.

Study and community work. They were the steady drumbeats, setting Marian's life on its path in her early years. Service, she would learn, was not something you did in your spare time; "it was the very purpose of life."

To keep his congregation informed about world and community events, the Reverend Wright spent only part of his sermons on the *Bible*. Often he would step down from the pulpit and talk with his parishioners. No topic was too small or too big. He would discuss the subject of cleanliness, how to care for gardens, and how the community must meet the needs of all its people: playgrounds and toys for young children, books for older children, and care for the sick and the elderly. Time and again, the Reverend Wright expressed the need to care for children. He described children as treasures who could flourish only if they had loving attention.

The minister used every occasion to bond religion to community life. In an article he wrote for a religious magazine, the *A. M. E. Zion Quarterly Review*, he said he felt his responsibility for the health of the community. "Helping children with physicians, medicines for the poor, [and] a playground" were essential to his work. He mentioned an experiment to have the church "house a clinic and a recreation center."

In a message to the Palmetto State Teachers Association, he wrote on the topic, "Education for Today's Children." "The biggest business in any society," he wrote, "is the nurturing, rearing, and cultivating of children." He called attention to the increase in broken homes, describing it as "the growing tragedy of our times. . . . The pressure of our high-powered civilization is too much for a homeless and loveless child. . . . Every child has a right to be loved," he wrote. The traditional fundamentals of the family and the home provide "a center of love," a nurturing environment to give children moral strength.

The Reverend and Mrs. Wright carried out their beliefs in their devotion to the community. There was the playground Marian's father built in back of the church so that African-American children would not feel left out of the segregated playgrounds. There was the time the minister literally scooped up the elderly parishioners suffering from the winter cold and lack of food and placed them in a building across from the church, starting the first home for old folk in the black community in South Carolina. To Mrs. Wright and the children fell the responsibility of cooking, cleaning, and caring for them. Marian would recall how eager she was to help, insisting when she was eight or nine that she was capable of washing and cleaning an elderly woman with bed sores.

These responsibilities were as much a part of Marian's life as "eating, breathing, and sleeping," she would say. The only bad thing about it was that "none of us learned to relax."

Another close childhood friend, Romaine Covington, recalled that Marian sometimes had to interrupt play to do chores. But she never complained. "Giving" was expected of her.

The giving worked two ways, creating a kinship in the community that

Marian, a young teenager, standing in her front yard on Cheraw Street

enriched everyone, especially the children. Each child felt protected in the large extended family, found every home open and every neighbor a friend and protector. Marian always remembered the feeling of being a child of the community, recounting that neighbors praised her when she did well in school and helped with chores. On the other hand, they chided her when she did something they considered wrong. She would always remember that the community caring helped create self-esteem in the children and gave them a sense of moral worth.

Though the African-American community in Bennettsville was strong; had created its own turf; and was in many ways self-sufficient with its own school, churches, and small businesses; it nevertheless was isolated from the mainstream. No matter how well it did, it did not have access to either money or power. Young people could laugh at, and many did, the strange ways of whites who demanded that blacks drink from one water fountain and they from another. A few daring youngsters would stealthily drink from a "whites only" water fountain to discover the water tasted the same. "How stupid!" they said, but the hurt did not go away. Deep down they questioned themselves. Are we lacking in something? For the few who escaped the poison of racist patterns, there were the many who could not make it, whose spirits were injured and deadened.

Those who succeeded, nevertheless, suffered a waste of creative talent. Many bright young people of Marian's age could not develop their potential as writers, artists, artisans, or leaders. Instead they directed their energies into survival skills, learning to deal with black and white worlds.

The surrounding community of white people practicing its racist policies "made her wild," Marian would say. A few experiences filled her with pain and rage, such as the time a car with a black migrant family collided with a white truck driver near Bennettsville. The ambulance took the slightly injured white truck driver to the hospital and refused to help the badly injured black migrant family. Or the time her schoolmate, Henry, jumped off the bridge into the town creek, where he thought he could swim, and broke his neck. He was not permitted to use the town pool. A hurt that haunted her was the childhood death of a neighbor, little Johnny, who had stepped on a nail and died because the family could not get proper medical care.

Countless events in her life were marked by prejudice and segregated facilities. After a time she refused to go to the town movie theater. It was too insulting to be sent up to the segregated balcony, she told her friend Ruth.

Even as a youngster, she was aware of racism and hated it. In the sixth grade she wrote an essay titled, "Barriers of Racial Injustice Do Not Have to Be Insurmountable." It was so impressive, said Ruth, that Marian was asked to read the essay at the school assembly. At the age of 11 or 12,

Marian had already decided that segregation was a terrible evil, Ruth recalled. Marian would say to her friend, "You know, I hate the idea of a segregated movie theater. And we can't go to the public library; and we can't sit at a lunch counter and have a Coke; and we can't do this and we can't do that. I'm going to do something about it."

By the time she reached her last year at the Marlboro Training High School, Marian was a slender young girl—bright, animated, and articulate. Schoolmates recall her as the brightest in the class. "Assign" herself she did. "She always read the whole book when the class was asked to read one chapter," a friend recalled. A few students were in awe of her, and to her embarrassment, she was often a teacher's pet, held up as a model student. An English teacher, holding up samples of Marian's penmanship for others to see, said to her class, "You can do what Marian Elizabeth does; you can do it." Only in sewing was she a slow learner. "She could barely sew a straight stitch," a teacher commented.

Marian, called "Redhead" in high school

The attention did not spoil Marian. She was outgoing and caring, able to identify with all members of her school class. Still, she was different, and her classmates understood that somehow Marian's future was bright with promise.

There were light moments when Marian, a majorette, twirled a baton at school functions, and when she and close friends were together, whispering and laughing over private matters.

The happy mix of her days was shattered when her father died suddenly in May 1954. She was with him in the ambulance on the way to the hospital. His final words were fixed in her mind, words that gave her confidence, gave her a sense of empowerment by assuring her that she, a black girl, could be anything she wanted to be. Education, self-discipline, and determination were important.

The Reverend Wright died ten days before the Supreme Court decision *Brown v. Board of Education of Topeka.* He had impatiently awaited the decision in the landmark case that finally overturned segregation in education.

Marian, in front, with school friends Romaine Covington, Douglas Gregg, and Ruth Thomas

By her last year in high school, Marian was the only child at home. Her sister, Olive, had graduated from Fisk University and had become a teacher of romance languages. Her brother Harry was at Colgate Seminary in Rochester, New York, and her other two brothers were at North Carolina Central College in Durham.

To make up for the empty household, Mrs. Wright—who already was the director of the old folks home—reached again into the community and took in foster children. In the extended family, the bedrooms were always occupied by youngsters whom Mrs. Wright wanted to help along, generously sharing what she had to offer with the less fortunate. Over the years, there would be twelve foster children in the Wright home. Mrs. Wright was "somehow angelic," a young member of the community would say.

Mrs. Wright holding twin foster children

The Maggie L Wright Home for Adult Care

Marian's senior year at high school was strewn with honors. Selected as brightest in her graduating class in 1956, she was the valedictorian and addressed the assemblage of parents, teachers, and county educators. The yearbook's prophecy foresaw her as a physician: "Dr. Marian E. Wright," who would be "praised for her amazing discoveries of painless obstetrics."

Marian E. Wright would often look back over the years and recognize those precious moments when she had been lifted out of the difficulties of being an African American in a white world. She would quote her father, who had reminded her that "nothing is too lowly for me to do," and that "the South's sickness in no way diminishes my intrinsic worth as a human being." She would recall the strength of her mother and the family, the

Marian, center (at typewriter), with members of 1956 yearbook
committee of Marlboro Training High School

church, and the community, as well as the support from teachers; the tal-
ented women who affirmed the worth of their students and helped them
ward off the bruises of the white world.

Religion would always be a part of her life. She was the niece, daughter,
and granddaughter of Baptist ministers and her brother Harry, who was
studying for the ministry, would later take her father's place in
Bennettsville's Shiloh Baptist Church.

She would always remember that she was God's child. As such she was
equal to everyone. She was no better and no worse. She could look down
on no one, and no one could look down on her.

CHAPTER FOUR

A Larger World

At 17 and ready for college, Marian's first choice was Fisk University in Nashville, Tennessee, where her sister, Olive, had studied. Her mother, however, wanted her youngest child closer to home and Spelman College in Atlanta, Georgia, which offered her a scholarship, seemed a desirable choice. Spelman was known as the largest liberal arts college in the country for black women.

But should she be going to an all-black school in 1956, two years after the *Brown* verdict desegregated education? Shouldn't she try to challenge a white college? Her two older brothers, Arthur and Harry, talked about it. Her mother, however, thought it was too risky because so much violence broke out when blacks tried to integrate schools. Again her mother's wish prevailed. In addition, Mrs. Wright pointed out that the family had friends in Atlanta.

In the fall of 1956, Marian and school friend Ruth Thomas were driven by their families to the small town of Hamlet, North Carolina, where they boarded a train that took them away from home.

Spelman's campus was cool and green, shaded by tall old trees and stands of magnolias. Two-story red-brick buildings housed classrooms, dormitories, and administration offices. More than its physical beauty, Spelman offered a safe haven. Within its confines, free of racism, students could devote themselves to their education and develop their creativity and leadership skills. The school also fostered a feeling of family by having students call one another "sister."

Along with a structured academic program Spelman trained its young women in the genteel tradition, emphasizing the need to be well mannered, poised, and respectful. Above all, students were urged to stay out of trouble. For their safety off campus, they were required to go in groups when riding into town to shop or just to walk around. White Atlantans found "the well-behaved Spelman students" models of deportment. They offered no challenge in 1956 to Atlanta's white supremacy.

Helping Spelman students to develop self-discipline were compulsory morning worship from Monday to Friday each week and

Packard Hall, a student dormitory and admissions office at Spelman College

Sisters Chapel, Spelman College

regular Sunday afternoon Vespers. Not only was attendance taken but proper dress for services was required. Marian, a late riser, was often seen rushing across the campus with her pajamas hanging down beneath a skirt she hastily put on.

Perhaps to please her mother, Marian started her college career majoring in music. After a few weeks, she changed over to biology to prepare for pre-medical studies. The illusion of wanting to become a physician lasted until she began to dissect frogs.

Though she went on to other studies, she never gave up music. Spelman had musicians in residence, and its choir was extraordinary, as was the small Morehouse choir made up of eight Morehouse men and eight Spelman women. Marian sang in both choirs throughout her college years, and she would always be grateful to her mother for her musical training.

With the usual trial and error of trying to decide on a suitable course of study, Marian finally settled on a major in history and social studies.

In that area she had her interest challenged by Dr. Howard Zinn, who became chairman of the History Department the year she entered Spelman. The two new arrivals created classroom excitement; she was eager to learn, he was eager to teach. She stood out immediately in the class on American history, bright, articulate, confident—the qualities she brought from home.

The students at Spelman were impressed with Marian's strong intellect and unpretentious personality. Despite her academic success and her easy friendships with faculty members, she had no airs and appeared to be quite ordinary.

A Spelman sister would talk about Marian's capacity to concentrate. "She had tremendous focus and single-mindedness of purpose," Roslyn Pope said. "She was not a social butterfly; [she was] not concerned with styles of dress or anything not relevant to what she considered important."

Another Spelman student, Joan Johnakin, who knew Marian in Bennettsville and was in her first year when Marian was a sophomore, said that Marian encouraged her when Joan was having difficulty with one of her classes. "You can make it," Marian would say. And "make it" Joan did, grateful for Marian's support and confidence in her.

Classmate Herschelle Sullivan remembered Marian as "persevering" and "not a traditional student but an independent spirit."

In a short time, she had the affection of her classmates and the esteem of her teachers. Dr. Zinn, in particular, found her winning for she was never arrogant or overbearing. He, a northern white with a recent doctorate from Columbia University, was filling his first full-time teaching position in Spelman's interracial teaching staff. He brought a brave new voice to Spelman. The racist South was something that had to be changed, and he would help his students challenge segregation by joining their struggles and sometimes by inspiring them.

Both students and teachers eagerly watched the progress of the Montgomery bus boycott in 1956, the year Marian entered Spelman. The leader of the movement, Martin Luther King, Jr., had been born and raised in Atlanta and was a Morehouse College graduate. His family lived there and his father was the well-known pastor of the Ebenezer Baptist Church. Christine King Farris, his sister, taught at Spelman. At the end of 1956, Dr. King would return to Atlanta to co-pastor his father's church.

In terms of race relations, Atlanta was called a "moderate" city. It carried out its segregationist policies and flew the Confederate flag but no violent confrontations broke its quiet. In fact, the city administration was flexible enough to permit small victories in the late fifties. The small victories brought small changes.

Marian had her first interracial experience at Spelman when she participated in seminars at the local Young Women's Christian Association. Still in her first year, she was one of Spelman's bold students and refused to take a back seat in Atlanta's segregated buses.

Professor Zinn took steps to break Atlanta's racist codes by encouraging his students to desegregate Atlanta's main library. Marian, or other students, would enter the large attractive downtown building and explain that a certain book was not available at her school. After the pressure of students from Spelman, Morehouse, and Atlanta's other black colleges, the library was opened to African Americans. The same sort of action desegregated the municipal auditorium.

On one occasion, Professor Zinn took his class to visit the Georgia State Legislature then in session. When they arrived, they spontaneously decided to desegregate the visitors' gallery. African-American students sat down among the whites. The audacity of their action brought the session to a standstill. The Speaker stopped the proceedings and ordered the Spelman students removed from the white section. The students found seats in the segregated part of the gallery, but in protest Professor Zinn sat with them, integrating it for that visit.

Though these flurries of excitement raised hopes, life in Atlanta remained segregated and stifling in its restraints. The bits and pieces of freedom did not change the basic structure. Marian had come to Spelman to learn and to grow, but she was aware from morning to night of the racist pattern and its humiliations. She was not free to choose a restaurant, to travel, or to go spontaneously into Atlanta just to walk around—or to vote or have a political voice. The anger and the frustration were muted, but they were there. Even a liberal professor could not compensate for the exhausting need to deal with racism on an intellectual level—to see the bias in books, never having your race portrayed as a realistic part of history.

All that changed for Marian when, at the end of her sophomore year, she won a Merrill Foreign Study-Travel grant to study in Europe her junior year. On the advice of Professor Zinn and other professors, she chose to go on her own rather than as part of a group. It gave her a sense of responsibility for her decisions. Her companion for parts of the trip was Virginia Powell, another Spelman student and Merrill scholarship winner.

Marian's mother and family, though anxious about her welfare, were fully supportive, and she left for Paris, France, on June 7, 1958. For the two summer months she studied at the Sorbonne. The idea of a career in the foreign service challenged her and she wanted more than classes in French civilization. To prepare for her new profession, she entered the University of Geneva in Switzerland and enrolled in a course of study in international relations.

Geneva's strong international life exhilarated her as much as the physical beauty of Lake Geneva surrounded by snow-capped mountains did. One of the oldest centers of learning in Europe, the University of Geneva celebrated its 400th anniversary that year. The student body was made

University of Geneva

up of young people from many countries; and, Marian reported, her contact with persons of "varied backgrounds, ideologies, and races afforded more valuable information of international relations than any course" could have given her.

Geneva was also the site for the meetings of the United Nations and more than 81 international bureaus. Marian attended many of these meetings and broadened her understanding of different peoples and ideas. More than intellectual exhilaration, life in Europe was giving her a sense of freedom, of strength, as though she were breathing clean air for the first time.

She traveled extensively during her 10 months in Geneva. Every opportunity, every school vacation, provided time to visit other countries. She made a tour of the British Isles, including Ireland and Scotland. She traveled to the Netherlands and Spain. During one holiday, she and three other students rented a car, a Volkswagen, and drove to southern France and Italy. The car, she wrote in a letter to Dr. Albert E. Manley, president of Spelman, "enabled us to go to many places . . . and in addition gave me a lot of confidence in my driving after surviving those 'hair-pin' mountains."

In a letter to Dr. Manley in mid-year, she wrote, "Time flies so! In pondering my stay in Europe I have been jolted to realize that I have already reached the 'half-way mark.' I am for the first time really feeling the importance of time. . . . I am learning to value each moment as a precious entity and to squeeze every possible amount of activity into it."

After her school year in Geneva, a Lisle Fellowship made it possible for her to spend the summer of 1959 in the then Soviet Union. The fellowship also provided for travel in Germany, Poland, and Czechoslovakia. The Soviet Union held special interest for her as the land of her favorite author, Leo Tolstoy. She also hoped to meet the noted African-American educator and author W. E. B. DuBois, who often spent long visits there, but he had already departed.

On her travels through the Soviet Union, Marian was joined by Spelman sister Virginia Powell who had also won a Lisle Fellowship. It was easy for the two young women to mix with the Soviet people whom they found to be friendly and inquisitive. A routine day they planned to spend at the World's Fair held in Moscow that summer turned into one of great excitement when they unexpectedly came across the official United States delegation. As U. S. students studying abroad, they attached themselves to the distinguished group headed by Vice President Richard Nixon and made up of diplomats and trade union and cultural leaders. Squired around by Soviet and U. S. experts, the group visited the many exhibits,

Marian, second from left, and Virginia, on left, with Premier Khrushchev

and during the day's celebrations Marian and Virginia caught a glimpse of the Soviet premier, Nikita Khrushchev.

Free to wander around, they visited historic sites and attended "hush-hush" church services, as Virginia Powell put it. Though religious practices were illegal, they nevertheless survived in underground or clandestine meetings.

Encounters with Russian students and the free interchange of ideas about their different cultures and languages were highlights of their Soviet travels. The Russians were curious about racial segregation in the United States and how the two African-American women managed their lives.

It was all a bit of a wonderland: mountain climbing with Russian students in the Crimea and then actually meeting Nikita Khrushchev. The premier was driving through the countryside with his aides and stopped to talk. He was pleasant, Virginia recalled, and invited Marian and her to stay on in the Soviet Union.

During her year in Europe, Marian saw its cultural treasures in the great museums: the Louvre in Paris, the Prado in Madrid, Leningrad's Hermitage, and others. She spoke to people everywhere: to the English as she walked along the Thames River, to the Dutch living in a windmill, to the Jews in a Warsaw ghetto, and to the people of Prague and Belgrade.

Seeing things with fresh eyes made Marian examine her own life. Not

Marian on right, Virginia Powell, center, resting after mountain climbing in the Caucuses near the Black Sea

only was she an individual but she was also a member of a world community, a larger world. She also recognized that she had become a fighter, ready to battle for things in which she believed. "I have seen and felt the suffering of others and gained incentive to alleviate it in my own small way," she wrote in an article for the *Spelman Messenger*, the school paper. In recognizing that she had changed and was part of a larger world, she also recognized that the struggle before her had become larger. Fighting for freedom and equality in the South of the United States had worldwide importance. Race relations, she now knew, would influence the health both economically and intellectually of the United States and affect its position in the world. About herself, she wrote, "I am no longer an isolated being. . . . I belong. Europe helped me to see this."

CHAPTER FIVE

"We Want to Walk into the Sun"

S HE CAME BACK A DIFFERENT PERSON," HER BROTHER Harry recalled when Marian arrived home in September 1959 after 15 months in Europe. Marian herself knew that Europe had been a "liberating experience," and that she had grown away from the racist southern way of life. For more than a year she had been a citizen of the world, moving freely through the different countries of Europe. She slept, ate, walked, and traveled wherever she chose. The daily humiliation of being an African American in the United States had dimmed. What a shock it was to return to the southern patterns of racism, to find them still there painfully intrusive and unyielding. "After a year's freedom as a person, I wasn't prepared to go back to a segregated existence," she said.

She may have completely outgrown segregation but the South clearly had not. Still, Spelman College was not the same as it had been when she returned there for her senior year. She found the campus alive with new student energy. Inroads had been made in desegregating the libraries, theaters, restaurants, and buses. There were more whites on campus due to a larger interracial teaching staff. And the college was planning to enroll its first white exchange student. But Atlanta basically remained a tightly segregated city.

Marian's impatience with racism reflected the way millions of others felt. African-American students on southern campuses increasingly resented their lack of personal, social, and political freedom. The time had come when they wanted to sit and eat wherever they chose to do so.

The constant humiliation, the slow pace of change, and the worry that things might never change compelled four students to say no to segregation in an unique way.

On February 1, 1960, four African-American students at A & T (Agricultural and Technical) State University in Greensboro, North Carolina, sat down at a lunch counter in the downtown Woolworth's. The store, like all others, was segregated but the four sat on counter stools and refused to leave when told that Negroes were not served. The students sat there for one hour. Management then closed the counter for the day, and the students left.

None of the students expected any publicity yet the event was picked up and broadcast throughout the nation by television, radio, and newspapers. The "sit-in," as it was called, had the most startling results. It became the topic of talk on college campuses and in families across the South. And it released torrents of pent-up rage among the young, leading to a wave of non-violent sit-ins across the country. By February 25, sit-ins had spread to other southern cities, among them Durham, Winston-Salem, Charlotte, Fayetteville, and Raleigh.

At Spelman, sophomore Ruby Doris Smith read about it and so did seniors Marian Wright, Roslyn Pope, Ruth Thomas, and many others. At Morehouse, journalism student Julian Bond and former Korean War veteran, and now a student, Lonnie King heard about it. Bond and King discussed the Greensboro sit-in and decided, yes, it was something they could do in Atlanta. Bond remembered the Montgomery bus boycott of 1955–1956 and the sacrifice Rosa Parks had made. Others also remembered the boycott; it helped "generate the movement of 1960," student leader James Forman would say.

Bond and King called a meeting of college students from the six black colleges making up the Atlanta University Center. These included Morehouse, Spelman, Clark, Morris Brown, Atlanta University (a graduate school), and the Interdenominational Theological Center.

Marian and Roslyn Pope were among the Spelman representatives at the student meeting, where it was decided to call for a sit-in on March 15. As a preliminary step, to appease administrative officials who were wary of the sit-in, the students agreed to place a full-page advertisement in the leading Atlanta newspapers. On March 9, 1960, such an ad appeared: AN APPEAL FOR HUMAN RIGHTS. It pointed out the areas of inequality in education, employment, housing, voting rights, medical care, and cultural opportunities. The students pledged their support for non-violent means such as sit-down demonstrations to gain their rights; rights "which are inherently ours as members of the human race and as citizens of these United States." Further, the Appeal stated, "Today's youth will not sit by submissively, while being denied all of the rights, privileges, and joys of life."

The Appeal brought shock and surprise to Georgia and other southern states. Daily life was not as smooth as it had been for white people. Hundreds of young African Americans had taken leadership into their own hands with the reasonable demand that they could also sit at a lunch counter and be served.

Committees were hard at work carefully planning the March 15 sit-ins.

Student leaders in 1960—from left: Julian Bond, Marian Wright, Lonnie King, and Ben Brown

The upsurge was gripping Atlanta's black students. In challenging the entrenched segregation, they were moving mountains. Even the genteel and traditional Spelman students felt the tremors of change. Marian, deeply involved in the action, posted a notice on her dormitory bulletin board announcing "Young ladies who can picket, please sign below." Students were given a choice of whether they would picket, sit-in and be arrested, or not. Marian was one of those who agreed to be arrested. Her mother, whom she had consulted, did not disagree with her decision. To prepare herself for a night in jail, Marian took with her a book, *The Screwtape Letters*, by C. S. Lewis.

Promptly at 11:30 A.M. on Tuesday, March 15, Marian and her group started their sit-in at the City Hall cafeteria. They were among 200 students who converged on ten target points in downtown Atlanta and sat down at eating places in public, tax-supported buildings. These included the public cafeterias at the state capitol, the county courthouse, two railway stations, and two bus stations.

It was the largest demonstration of its kind staged in the South. The next day the *Atlanta Constitution* announced in leading headlines, 77 NEGROES ARRESTED IN STUDENT SITDOWNS AT 10 EATING PLACES HERE. Marian Wright was among the 14 Spelman students arrested and jailed. After a few hours, she and the others were released on bail.

Student picketing spread to retail stores and to chain grocery stores with the demand that they increase the number of African-American employees.

Atlanta had never seen such political activism. Nor had its citizens ever expected to see young African-American students, clear about what they were doing, walk into public facilities and demand equal rights.

Even those not sympathetic at first to the cause could not help but admire the goal of the demonstrators and their non-violent tactics. Atlanta's police were careful. The city administrators did not want to spoil Atlanta's image as a peaceful town.

Marian had her first real taste of a movement for social change and she was soon caught up in the excitement, tensions, and camaraderie. She could see the demands for change blow like a whirlwind through the South. By April, there were sit-ins in 125 cities. On May 17, she was among the 1,500 students who marched through downtown Atlanta to the Wheat Street Baptist Church for a mass meeting to celebrate the sixth anniversary of the Supreme Court decision in 1954 desegregating schools.

The urgency of the struggle made her shift her plans for the future. No longer was she interested in studying the Russian language and international relations for a career in the foreign service. Her help was needed in her own country, and that became painfully clear when she volunteered during the afternoons at the local branch of the National Association for the Advancement of Colored People (the NAACP). In her job to look over complaints that came into the office, she saw that poor people, black people, could not get legal help because many white lawyers would not take civil rights cases. Upset at the situation, she decided to study law, not because she felt a special interest in becoming an attorney but because the law could be a useful tool in the fight against segregation.

She was accepted at Yale Law School, winning a John Hay Whitney Foundation Fellowship and a Yale University Law School scholarship for the first year of study.

During her final months at Spelman, she moved in militant activist student circles and knew the young leaders. At that time Ella Baker was the head of the Atlanta branch of the Southern Christian Leadership Conference (SCLC). Baker, a brilliant strategist, knew the time was ripe for a new organization. Students were already shaking up the South with their sit-ins, and she thought it important that they have an opportunity to develop their own movement and tactics without the influence of an older conservative leadership.

She called a conference for Easter weekend, April 15–17, 1960, at Shaw University in Raleigh, North Carolina. Attending it were over 200 delegates representing 58 southern communities and 19 northern colleges. Out of the conference came a new organization, the Student Non-Violent Coordinating Committee (SNCC).

The movement is a protest and it is an affirmation, SNCC said in its opening statement. *We want to recognize our potential. We want to walk into the sun and through the front door.*

The auditorium was hot that April when the students all rose to sing "We Shall Overcome," the song that would become the national anthem of the civil rights movement. "It was the beginning . . . and it was the purest moment," Jane Stembridge, a white student and SNCC's first secretary, said.

Over the months, SNCC would use a new code word: "civil disobedience," said Dr. Howard Zinn in his book SNCC: *The Student Non-Violent Coordinating Committee.* He called it a way to "confront policymakers directly with a power beyond orthodox politics—the power of people in the streets and on the picket line!"

In the spring of 1960, Marian, an honor student and again class valedictorian, graduated from Spelman. Her family came for commencement exercises. They cheered the youngest among them, who was now a college graduate too. Before entering Yale in the fall, she had a summer job at a research organization in the vicinity of Washington, D.C.

Until the end of her days at Spelman, she attended meetings called by the Raleigh Conference group. In May 1960, the first meeting was held on the campus of Atlanta University. Among the 15 student leaders present was Marian. But she was leaving an Atlanta now engulfed in student activism. The breakdown of old codes of behavior and a vision of the new—of freedom and equality—called for her and for tens of thousands of others to join the struggle.

The state of her mind, the overstress of her many undertakings, is revealed in a letter she wrote on June 4, 1960, from Spelman College to Ella Baker. She had not compiled a report about the Raleigh Conference as she had promised, she wrote. The notes had been sent home with other "school materials" earlier in the week. She planned to return home to Bennettsville to attend to "many loose ends," after which she would be back in Atlanta to attend a meeting. "I do want to impress upon you," she wrote, "that I am not usually so undependable as I have proved with the Raleigh report."

Marian, 1960, a Spelman College graduate with friends Fred Bell, Jr., of Morehouse and Ruth Thomas

CHAPTER SIX

The Yale Years

IN HER FIRST TWO YEARS AT YALE LAW SCHOOL, MARIAN found her classes more a chore than a pleasure. She hated "the whole course of study," she told journalist Calvin Tomkins for his 1989 *New Yorker* magazine profile. "I'd had no idea what law school was going to be like, and the one thing I looked forward to during those years was never having to read cases again." The cut-and-dry legal language seemed unconnected to what was happening around her and she found it difficult to concentrate on her studies. What excited her at Yale was the upsurge in political activism, the many bold students and teachers speaking out on civil rights, and in that circle she made good friends.

Northern campuses in support of the civil rights struggles in the South became centers of political movements. From Berkeley, California, to Cambridge, Massachusetts, students burst out of their cocoons of silence to join the fight for equality for African Americans.

Yale was the home base for the northern student movement, and that's where field organizer Bob Moses came to speak. The Harlem-born 25-year-old Moses had a Harvard graduate degree in philosophy and had given up his job teaching mathematics at the prestigious Horace Mann School in New York City to work full-time for SNCC.

In the summer of 1960, soon after SNCC was formed, Moses traveled through the South to recruit young people for a conference to be held in Atlanta. By 1961, he had set up a voter registration project in Mississippi which had the lowest percentage of black voter registration in the

Yale Law School

South. He worked out of an office in Greenwood, a cotton growing center in Leflore County and, along with Sunflower County, the most violent area in the state.

Within a short time, Bob Moses was shot at, beaten, arrested, and jailed. Nothing deterred him. His commitment to change the South only deepened.

From time to time Moses came North to talk to students and to raise funds. His Harvard graduate friends developed a support network, and through the Harvard group Marian got to know him. From her friendship with him and his talks to students, she learned about conditions in Mississippi—about the aroused Ku Klux Klan and the development of another hate group. The White Citizens Council, formed in the small

49

town of Indianola, was launched to fight against any changes in segregation after the 1954 Supreme Court decision. She learned about the poverty and powerlessness of the African Americans and the stirrings of hope. Moses spoke movingly about the courage of ordinary people who tried to register to vote knowing the price they might pay in lost jobs, lost homes, beatings, and possibly murder.

Another speaker who inspired Marian was the political leader Malcolm X, who addressed a crowded auditorium at Yale Law School in early 1960. She found him "mesmerizing," "brilliant," "funny." "He expressed the rage that all of us continued to feel about the slow pace of change in the country, but he did it in the cleverest and the funniest way you could imagine," she said. He gave a different point of view, a strategy different from Dr. King's advocacy of non-violence in the struggle for social change. "Even though we believed in non-violence, it was also very good to have somebody vent the other side," was her comment.

Though she attended her classes, Marian's mind and heart were in the struggles for freedom. Sharing her feelings was the Reverend William Sloane Coffin, Jr., the Yale University chaplain with whom Marian had become friends and in whose home she lived for a year as a member of the family. Dr. Coffin was an early Freedom Rider, one of those courageous people who faced brutal violence to challenge segregation in interstate travel in the Deep South. When Marian wanted to join him on a Freedom Ride, he would not permit it knowing its dangers.

She helped Dr. Coffin, however, on a local project. By becoming the first black woman usher at Yale's Batelle Chapel, she desegregated the group by both race and gender.

She was involved not only with the struggles here at home, but also in Africa where countries were winning their independence from colonial rule and reclaiming their own culture and nationhood.

Marian Wright among the 1962 Crossroaders on the South Lawn
of the White House to hear President Kennedy's greetings
To the left of the President: Senator Hubert Humphrey and
Crossroads Director the Reverend James H. Robinson

In her eagerness to be of service, she traveled to Africa in the summer of 1962. Through a national organization, Operation Crossroads Africa, she became one of some 300 student participants sent across the African continent for study-work projects. Inspired by the rising tide of independence of many African nations, the Crossroaders wanted to help rebuild these countries. Marian, one of three African Americans in a group of 11, spent two months in the Ivory Coast, a small agricultural country that declared its independence from France in 1960. The students came prepared to do physical labor—to restore schools, hospitals, churches, and roads. Marian and her group at first were assigned to build a school, but that project changed course and she spent the summer building a reinforced concrete fence that was to surround a school.

A highlight of the summer was a trip to Ghana, the neighboring country to the east. Along with her colleagues, she traveled by truck over bumpy roads to Ghana's capital city, Accra. The students hoped to get a broader view of Africa by seeing the effects of colonialism in two countries that had similar indigenous cultures but were ruled by different foreign nations: the Ivory Coast by France and Ghana by England. Under the leadership of the African nationalist Kwami Nkrumah, Ghana became an independent republic in 1960.

On her return after the exhilarating but arduous summer, Marian entered her third and final year at Yale Law School. Her courses set, she again became immersed in the continuing civil rights struggles at home. In the spring of 1963, she decided to go to Mississippi to join the voter registration drive. As was her custom, she discussed her plans with her mother who, always concerned about her safety, made Marian promise she would not get into trouble and she would not get arrested.

She flew to Jackson where Medgar Evers, NAACP field secretary in Mississippi, met her. He drove her some 96 miles north to Greenwood, the headquarters for SNCC and other civil rights groups. It was here that Bob Moses met Amzie Moore in 1960, and the two decided to work together on voter registration. Moore—a World War II veteran, postal worker, gas station owner, and president of the Cleveland branch of the NAACP—was bold and fearless. When he and Moses launched their new project, they set in motion an irresistible force that made Mississippi the heartbeat of an emerging movement. They settled into their work, as the Negro spiritual says, "like a tree planted by the water" and they would "not be moved."

The Delta was an unique stretch of land, home to the greatest number of black people in the state, if not in the nation. The vast oval-shaped region was fertile, flat, and dense with cotton fields. Its soil was perpetually enriched by the material laid down in the yearly overflow of surrounding rivers: the Mississippi, the Yazoo, and the Tallahatchie. The thousands working as tenant farmers and laborers, combined with the long humid summers and the fertile soil, made the region profitable for white farmers. Through terror and violence, they kept the farm population poor and politically powerless.

In the three days she was there, Marian saw the leaders at work. She knew Bob Moses, and she met James Forman, the hardworking SNCC executive director and former Chicago teacher and journalist, as well as Aaron Henry, a pharmacist and NAACP leader, and others.

By the spring of 1963, the success in voter registration had aroused the lethal hatred of the Ku Klux Klan, who stepped up its violence, hoping to end the growing upsurge by forcing the leaders to leave town. But the courageous, bright young leaders withstood the bloody clubbings and jail terms and continued their relentless fight to force open the closed society.

Marian witnessed their courage. Could she deal with the barrage of violence? She heard about the explosives thrown into Aaron Henry's home and pharmacy store, about the shots that tore through a car in which three civil rights workers were traveling. The night before she arrived, an arsonist burned the SNCC office to the ground, destroying all its records and equipment. Then came her own baptism by fire.

On March 26, shots were fired into the Greenwood home of SNCC worker George Greene. His three children were not hurt though the shots ripped open their bedroom wall. To protest the shooting and to urge an end to literacy tests for voters, Bob Moses and Jim Forman led a group of about 100 people from a church meeting to the county courthouse. Marian was in the march with men, women, and children, singing freedom songs. She was at the end of the line behind an elderly man on crutches when she saw the police appear wearing yellow helmets, carrying riot sticks, and leading a police dog. She knew that Bob Moses was afraid of dogs; he had explained during a walk she once took with him that dogs had not been a part of his upbringing. But she saw Bob march on resolutely as the growling dog leaped at him and ripped apart his pants. People ran in all directions while the police arrested Bob, Jim, and others. As they were led away, one of them threw the car keys to Marian. She did not know what to do or whom to call. The name John Doar came to mind. He was the head of the civil rights division of the United States Department of Justice in Washington, D.C.

Agitated, Marian tried to describe to Doar the violent police attack on a peaceful line of people. Then she tried to get in touch with a local lawyer only to learn that the three black lawyers in all of Mississippi practiced in Jackson, almost a hundred miles away. She was not permitted into the courthouse to see what was happening. Through an open side door she heard that Moses, Forman, and their colleagues were being tried that day. Until money could be raised for bail, they would be held in jail.

That was when Marian confirmed her decision "to become a lawyer."

She had seen ordinary people risking their lives. What about people like her who had skills? Shouldn't they try to help? Shouldn't they offer their skills and talents to the fight?

After graduation from Yale, she won one of two internships with the NAACP Legal Defense Fund which had set aside scholarship money to train young lawyers to work in the South. At the end of the year the Inc Fund, as it was called, guaranteed salaries to the interns to work wherever they chose. Marian decided to open an office in Jackson, Mississippi.

CHAPTER SEVEN

The Magnolia State

*T*HOUGH REPORTS FROM MISSISSIPPI CONTINUED TO describe the terrible violence in what was called the Magnolia state, Marian did not waver in her decision to go there.

In 1961 Bob Moses, writing from a cell in the Magnolia County jail, called the early days of the struggle "a tremor in the middle of the iceberg." By 1964, the tremor had become a militant liberation struggle. Mississippi had been the focal point for four years of brilliant, persistent, and courageous activists who had inspired and led the state's 900,000 African Americans in a mass non-violent movement that continued to shake the old power structure with demands for full equality. Nothing less would do.

Murder and beatings continued. In 1963 Marian's friend, 39-year-old Medgar Evers, NAACP field secretary, was gunned down in the driveway of his home.

Marian, however, could also count the victories. In 1961 the Freedom

Rides had forced open segregated public transportation facilities in bus and railway stations. In the fall of 1962, James Meredith had won a harrowing victory when he, a black student, gained admission to the all-white University of Mississippi. The presence of the National Guard on campus was required to ensure his safety.

There were other victories when African-American children faced the scorn and hatred of white children, parents, and teachers in order to attend better schools. They had won that right in the 1954 *Brown* decision that desegregated education. Sometimes the victories were reversed when white parents withdrew their children from these schools and placed them in private educational facilities.

Above all, persistent voter registration efforts had led to an increase in the voting rolls by about a half of a million black votes.

Evolving from these victories was the development of an African-American leadership. Many people—long passive and submissive—talked up, made decisions, and became inspiring leaders and national figures. Everyone knew Mrs. Fannie Lou Hamer and Mrs. Victoria Gray. Working along with seasoned leaders like Aaron Henry, they challenged the regular Democratic Party of Mississippi. In April 1964, they organized the Mississippi Freedom Democratic Party (MFDP) and opened an office in Jackson. The fledgling party broke into the spotlight when it demanded to be seated at the Democratic National Convention.

By the time Marian opened an office for the NAACP Legal Defense and Education Fund in Jackson in the spring of 1964, a tested and experienced leadership existed; a leadership that had placed the struggle for freedom and equality on the national agenda. She joined forces with activists Bob Moses, James Forman, Amzie Moore, Aaron Henry, David Dennis, Lawrence Guyot, Mrs. Fannie Lou Hamer, and many others.

The Inc Fund was housed in a series of small rooms in the black sec-

Jackson, Mississippi, June 1963: Whites pour sugar, ketchup, and mustard over heads of restaurant lunch counter sit-in demonstrators.

tion of town. Sharing the space with Marian was colleague Henry Aronson and a staff of one. Immediately she had a full docket of cases getting people out of jail. Since she could not take the Mississippi bar exam until she had been a resident of the state for one year, she did all the preparatory work. The three black lawyers in town cooperated with her and argued her cases in state or county courts. She argued her own cases in federal court. After a year, to her surprise and delight, she passed the exam and became the first African-American woman admitted to the Mississippi bar.

Mrs. Fannie Lou Hamer at 1964 Democratic National Convention in Atlantic City, New Jersey

Marian opened her office in time to see a new project called the Mississippi Freedom Summer unfold in 1964. Under a coalition of leading organizations called COFO, or the Council of Federated Organizations, SNCC, the Congress of Racial Equality (CORE), SCLC, the NAACP, and leading members of the African-American community launched a nationwide initiative to bring students from all over the country to Mississippi to work on voter registration and other projects. The volunteers, who would be housed with black families, had to pay their own expenses. Answering the call were some 700 mostly white, middle-class students from Ivy League colleges and large universities.

To round out the project, COFO invited people of goodwill to come to Freedom Summer. The call brought church leaders, health workers, lawyers, and teachers. Groups came to Mississippi from the NAACP Legal

Defense Fund, the National Lawyers Guild, and the Lawyers Constitutional Defense Committee. COFO brought medical and dental personnel from the newly formed Medical Committee for Human Rights. They opened clinics to provide health care for the people of Mississippi and the volunteers. The Delta Ministry of the National Council of Churches was there. Educators arrived and worked out curriculum for the 41 Freedom schools that taught black history and literacy and helped people register to vote. Musicians, actors, and writers came to share their talents. Everyone had one goal: to change Mississippi and move it forward, away from its semi-feudal conditions.

Before the project could get underway, training classes for the volunteers were held at Western College for Women in Oxford, Ohio. The classes were to prepare the students for the tense atmosphere and the dangers they would encounter and also to instruct them in the use of non-violent resistance.

Flooded with work and adjusting to a new city, a new job, and a house of her own, Marian nevertheless took a few days' leave from her Jackson office and went to Oxford to attend the sessions. Child psychiatrist Robert Coles of Harvard University Health Service was there and he recalled meeting her. He saw her as a mature young woman, who was neither shy nor fearful. "She had good judgment, a sharp, active mind, and she knew how to stay connected to the ordinary people of the region," Cole told *New Yorker* journalist Calvin Tomkins. There was about her "a kind of lovely innocence. It's a mixture of gentleness and personal dignity and savvy," Coles recalled. "She didn't fall prey to arrogance or smugness."

While classes were in session in Oxford, three civil rights workers, CORE members Michael Schwerner and James Chaney, and newly arrived New Yorker Andrew Goodman, had gone in a van to investigate the site of a burned-down black church near Philadelphia, Mississippi. They were picked up by Deputy Sheriff Cecil Price. Several hours later they were released but they were never again seen alive.

The disappearance of the young civil rights workers at the beginning of the Freedom Summer project warned the students of the dangers they faced. A few returned home but most stayed on "to fight the evil system," as one student put it.

The disappearance of the three young men and the public outcry brought federal investigators to the scene. The nation, finally alerted to the Mississippi way of life, awoke each day to brutal headlines. The publicity notwithstanding, violence in Mississippi escalated. Six black churches were burned to the ground at the beginning of the summer of 1964, and there would be 27 destroyed by fire before the summer was over. Eighty civil rights workers were beaten and 1,000 arrested. Shots were fired into vehicles carrying students and staff, as well as into homes and shops. The Klan mustered its forces, riding through the dark roads at night.

The violence did not stop the movement but the air was charged with danger. White students living with black families drove the racists wild. They could not tolerate the mixing of races.

The newcomers and the experienced were on the alert and took precautions to safeguard their lives. On the surface, the countryside looked serene: an unbroken vista of cotton fields, here and there the shacks of farm workers, and deep inland the large columned homes of planters.

Immersed in the tireless round of case work, Marian Wright had become part of the great drama of events. She witnessed scenes where people who tried to register to vote were fired from their jobs and thrown out of their homes and off the land. These people, among them women like Mrs. Fannie Lou Hamer, inspired her. They were ordinary poor black folk but they had extraordinary courage and persistence.

She saw how many of those arrested were beaten in jail, their bones broken and their teeth cracked. In her early days, a young man was murdered in jail and she had to take his parents to view the body on which an autopsy had been performed. The painful experience gave her nightmares for weeks and at the same time strengthened her. "It's amazing what you can come to accept as part of your life," she said. She felt she could now face anything.

Aware of the dangers around her, she was vigilant, took the customary precautions, and then hoped for the best. When she traveled to other regions of the state, especially to the Delta, she was sure to leave the Leflore and the Sunflower counties before dark. Before entering her car, she checked it for bombs and she drove at night as little as possible. When she did, she was sure the lights were off in the car and the gas tank full. She had become so skilled in safety measures that she could spot a sheriff's car a mile in front of her and a mile in back of her.

She knew one thing—she could not give into fear. She learned to deal with it as she learned to deal with her anger and her rage; to put them at the service of the work she was doing. That work increased in scope when she came face to face with the profound problems and the savage cruelty that hung over the African Americans in Mississippi.

She worried about what would happen at the end of August, when the Freedom Summer project drew to a close and hundreds of white students left Mississippi. What would happen to the African Americans who had spoken up, who had raised their voices?

Marian stayed in Jackson doing her work. She was there, like the early leaders, for the long struggle. With Henry Aronson she handled the deluge of civil rights cases resulting from voter registration. She was besieged as well by cases ranging from school desegregation suits, equal employment and equal welfare payments for blacks, to integration of hospitals, restaurants, and other public facilities.

Lifelong habits were formed in those days. She could work with little sleep. Four or five hours sustained her as did a large breakfast of "grits, sausage, eggs, and coffee," she told Ponchitta Pierce of *Ebony* magazine.

After a couple of years in Mississippi, she not only worked hard but demanded the same of her small staff, and for that matter, of any volunteers who came to help. But the accumulated stress affected her. She was thin and tense and found it increasingly difficult to relax. Her impatience sometimes brought comments. She "appears to be rough with people . . . doesn't care what people think, thinks every Negro should be on the front line!" wrote H. Sullivan in *Ebony* magazine. She really did *not* care what people thought. Conditions had to change and she was busy doing just that.

When the pressure and stress were too much and she had to be alone, she closeted herself in the small comfortable house she had bought when she first arrived in Mississippi and did simple chores. Occasionally, she escaped to New York to spend time with old friends. But the black community needed her, trusted her, and made her feel at home. The Reverend Allen Johnson, pastor of Jackson's Pratt Methodist Church, said, "Marian is dedicated. She could do much better elsewhere, both socially and legally. We know her life is in danger. She is not from Mississippi, but we claim her as one of our own. She belongs to the new South."

A different set of problems moved into focus when Marian witnessed the profound poverty of the people. She could hardly believe what she saw. Many were near starvation and the conditions of the children were pitiful. Not only in the Delta but in the hills east and south of the Delta she found people who, forced off the land by mechanization, tried to survive on the income from small fields of cotton and a few cows and chickens. What was the good of desegregating a lunch counter, she wanted to know, if a person did not have the money to buy a cup of coffee?

CHAPTER EIGHT

"I'm Broke and I'm Hungry ..."

*P*OVERTY AND THE POOR HAD BECOME CENTRAL CONCERNS of the United States government in the early 1960s. To the general public it came as a shock to learn that behind the affluence and the show of grandeur millions of people lived at a poverty level.

In 1962, author Michael Harrington helped bring poverty to the public's attention with his book, *The Other America: Poverty in the United States*. In it, Harrington delivered the startling message that 40 to 50 million people in the United States were poor. These nameless men, women, and children were stuck away in the valleys of Appalachia, the rural South, suburban areas, and large cities. They were "invisible" to middle-class Americans, said Harrington, because they were quiet about their condition, and because they had no political voice. They lived their uncertain lives in the midst of the richest and most powerful country in the world.

Nowhere was poverty more marked and more painful than in Mississippi, the heart of the Deep South, where segregation, police brutality, and powerlessness kept millions deadened by hunger and pain. Whitney Young of the National Urban League called Mississippi "the bottom of the heap."

The civil rights movement brought the hunger in Mississippi to the public's attention. Though voter registration was the goal, civil rights workers lived with poor black families and saw the malnutrition and disease. They saw children suffering from soft deformed bones called rickets and from bleeding gums because of scurvy. They saw children with skinny legs and bloated bellies; children who never saw a doctor or a dentist; children who were listless and passive, their eyes dulled. Not only were many physically diseased but poverty robbed them of a sense of play, of joy.

The natural beauty of Mississippi did not escape the eye of the poor nor did it change the way they were forced to live. They grew up on the wide fertile plains and along the waterways that flowed into the Mississippi River. The birds and small wild animals that filled the wetlands sometimes provided a meal for them. And they worked the long day under the immense blue sky and the red-setting sun.

As sharecroppers, they rented a piece of land under a system in which the plantation owner lent them money for seed and tools. In return, the sharecroppers shared their produce with the plantation owner and somehow always remained in debt. "Sharecropping and being hungry went together," said the writer William Attaway. The scholar W. E. B. DuBois called the conditions of black sharecroppers a "shadow of slavery."

The people were tied to the land not only because on it they eked out their bare subsistence but because in a way it belonged to them. Their forefathers and foremothers created the farmland. They had cleared the jungles, drained the swamps, and built the levees that held back the rampaging Mississippi River. Farm workers knew no other world than the one that kept them out of school and put them in the fields at ages six and seven to pick cotton. They grew into a life that did not allow them to vote, think, eat, or grow.

Still, they did not crumble. They leaned on old traditions and lived together in extended families. They had their churches, and within their communities there were moments for laughter and wit.

They also had their music; not only gospel, but the blues, which found its way into bars and alleys and shacks. On drum, guitar, and harmonica, or on whatever instrument they could devise, musicians put words to haunting melodies and told about hunger, pain, and loneliness. "I'm broke and I'm hungry, ragged, and dirty, too," sang blues musician William Brown.

Marian Wright heard the music and she saw the poverty in her travels around the state. On her field trips into the rural areas of Mississippi to carry out her casework on integration and civil and legal rights, she visited the crowded homes and noticed the shattered windows, the sagging porches, and leaking roofs. She saw the hunger and pain of children kept from school so that they could work on the farms, or because they had no clothes for school. Something connected, surfaced: Freedom meant not only the right to vote but the right to decent jobs, homes, education, and medical care.

From her early days in Mississippi she realized jobs and education were important for the poor, but the extreme poverty she witnessed drove home the urgency for immediate action. Her fears were confirmed when she investigated conditions in the Delta and the surrounding hills and learned that some families of eight had an average yearly income of $215.

Reports on poverty had already reached the White House. During his brief years in office, President John Kennedy planned to deal with the problem. In August 1963, he observed the march of 250,000 people on Washington demanding "Jobs and Freedom," and he heard Martin Luther

King, Jr., declare, "I have a dream." Kennedy was putting together a task force to develop anti-poverty programs when he was assassinated in November 1963.

President Lyndon Johnson, following Kennedy into office, rescued the concept. In his first State of the Union Address, in March 1964, he called for a national war on poverty, reaffirming government responsibility. That same year the president won congressional passage of the Economic Opportunity Act. Among its benefits was a program for pre-school children called Operation Head Start, which would provide basic skills and health and nutritional services to the three-fourths of a million pre-school children from ages three to five living in disadvantaged families. The investment in the growth and development of poor children, it was hoped, would enable them to enter kindergarten on an equal footing with other children. The anti-poverty programs also introduced Medicaid, food stamps, and child nutrition benefits.

Medical examinations at a Head Start group

Mississippi children picketing in front of White House
for Head Start funds

The new federal programs were opposed in Congress by Mississippi's two senators. James O. Eastland and John Stennis refused to apply for Head Start funds for their state. Senator Stennis, worried that such programs would lead to integrated activities, tried to block passage of the entire anti-poverty bill. A greater fear than racial integration was the possibility that African Americans would get an education, and who knew where that might lead.

In the meantime, word had spread in the poor communities of Mississippi about the Head Start programs. Local groups gathered together to try to figure out how to get funded. Once the idea of government help got a foothold, increasing numbers of people and organizations—churches, civil rights groups, and schools—met and talked. Out of the meetings grew an umbrella organization called the Child Development Group of Mississippi, known as CDGM. At the head of the new organization were psychologist Tom Levin, a civil rights activist and a founder of the Medical Committee for Human Rights, and the Reverend Arthur Thomas of the Delta Ministry of the National Council of Churches.

CDGM wrote innovative proposals for Head Start programs and won $1.5 million in federal funding for the summer of 1965. The main office was set up in Mount Beulah, an abandoned black junior college located in the small town of Edwards 26 miles from Jackson. Housing was already underway in Mount Beulah for farmworkers forced off the plantations because of voter registration activities or because new technology reduced the number of available jobs.

Marian, who had settled into Jackson the previous spring, knew of the efforts to get Head Start funded. She had agreed to serve on the CDGM Board and to act as its counsel. But her agenda was overflowing. By the time Head Start was in operation, the Voting Rights Act was passed in August 1965 guaranteeing to *all* citizens the right to vote. Putting the Act into practice required a continued struggle. Marian was busy with new cases in addition to the heavy load of the civil rights and integration cases she had previously undertaken. Still, the excitement and enthusiasm over Head Start programs had reached her.

Under Levin's leadership, CDGM encouraged projects deep within the poor communities and gave the poor themselves a voice in planning and running the programs. Creative energies were released. Parents, who had never had a voice in dealing with their or their children's lives, began to speak up. Many were trained by CDGM staff to work on the new programs. They learned the techniques of educating three- to five-year-olds through songs, stories, and the use of colors and toys. Children were learning to laugh and play together, and they were learning they were important. In a few short weeks, 86 Head Start centers were set up throughout the state, placing over 10,000 children in preschool programs and giving jobs to 1,200 people. The creative and flexible programs had unexpected results in providing literacy training for adults and in opening centers for job and career planning. African Americans, represented on the CDGM Board, took an active role in decisions.

As Senator Stennis had predicted, the successful projects set off a new chain of events. Not only were classes and staffing interracial, but black people were becoming leaders. They began to ask questions: Why could they not have better schooling after Head Start? And better medical care, paved streets, and garbage removal?

Upset by the new developments, Senator Stennis used his high office in Congress to block additional money for Head Start programs for CDGM, whose funds ran only to September. He attacked the group in Mount Beulah for instigating racial strife, and he criticized the careless administrative procedures and claimed that funds were being misused.

To win refunding, Stennis demanded that CDGM move from Mount Beulah to Mary Holmes Junior College, an isolated site 200 miles away in the corner of the state. He also demanded changes in staffing and the tightening of financial procedures.

Marian, on the CDGM Board from the beginning but busy with other matters, either did not attend meetings or she arrived late. At the time, she was also on the Boards of the Delta Ministry and the Citizens Crusade Against Poverty, a trade-union-backed organization. She had become close friends at the Delta Ministry with Art Thomas, an original cosponsor with Tom Levin of CDGM.

Discussion at CDGM Board meetings developed into heated controversy about how to meet Senator Stennis's attacks and get the money to keep the Head Start programs going. Everyone agreed that Tom Levin was an inspirational leader. Marian, among others, admired him. Nevertheless, she was angry and frustrated by what she called "soft" administrative procedures and chaotic record-keeping. CDGM, precisely because it was doing such a good job, was "in a touchy situation," she said. The organization must be tightly directed and run and accountable for everything it did, she insisted. Even though no financial abuse had taken place, still every penny spent needed to be accounted for. For example, staff members who did not do their jobs, including former civil rights activists, had to be let go.

Some thought Marian was critical of the very quality of CDGM that had made it so successful, its flexibility and looseness. In later years, Marian would praise CDGM for being an exciting and innovative program in participatory democracy and for giving poor African Americans an opportunity to direct their own lives. In the summer of 1965, however, when CDGM was fighting for funds, she was tough and became a forceful voice. As a board member and counsel to CDGM, she insisted on drastic changes in order, she said, to provide the poor with the best possible protection because people out there were "picking" on them.

The controversy spilled into the communities. Many supported Levin's approach and were willing to run the programs without government funding so the programs could remain community-based. Others backed Marian's proposals to make changes that would win government refunding of Head Start.

The arguments never were over dedication to the poor but about how to administer the programs that benefited them. Where was the center of power? Tom Levin urged that community people, parents in schools and churches, run and develop the programs with whatever mistakes they might make.

Marian, on the other hand, called for a tightly controlled central leadership that would be held responsible for everything, including developments on a community level. Accountability was of paramount importance.

Out of the intense organizational wrangling emerged a new leader. Marian had successfully moved the organization in the direction she thought necessary. That direction would mean continued government support of programs for the poor.

Even though Tom Levin was scheduled to leave CDGM in September and return to private practice, he was relieved of his job as director three weeks early. Marian replaced Levin with her Harvard friend John Mudd. The CDGM offices were moved from Mount Beulah to Jackson. In time, procedures were tightened and put in order. Changes were made in staffing and accountability. Notwithstanding the changes and Marian's leadership, CDGM did not win refunding until February 1966.

The struggles within CDGM and the need to fight for refunding for Head Start focused Marian's attention in a new direction. She had been concerned about hungry children from her early days in Mississippi. In discussions with Art Thomas and the Delta Ministry, she had envisioned a program that would help children medically and educationally. When she saw the success of Head Start for both children and parents, she knew the importance of government responsibility and its funding of programs benefiting the poor.

Mademoiselle magazine recognized Marian Wright's strong voice and leadership, and in January 1966 chose her as "one of four most exciting young women in the country." Each one of the four, said the award, had "brought to her field an outstanding degree of dedication and skill."

Marian in her mid-twenties in Mississippi, 1966

Marian Wright receives the congratulations of Harrison E. Salisbury of the *New York Times* on receiving a *Mademoiselle* magazine Annual Merit Award.

Marian was prepared to fly to New York to participate in the award ceremonies but a demanding legal case kept her in Mississippi.

Ebony magazine also called national attention to Marian's leadership. In June 1966, journalist Ponchitta Pierce wrote a major story, "The Mission of Marian Wright," describing Marian's work among poor Mississippi blacks and conditions of life in the Delta.

CHAPTER NINE

"Empty Cupboards . . ."

THE MONUMENTAL CIVIL RIGHTS ACTIVISM LEADING TO the passage of the Voting Rights Act in 1965 did not change economic conditions in Mississippi. But Marian Wright had become a voice to be reckoned with on the dangers of poverty and hunger and the need for government help.

In seeking solutions to farm poverty, she won in 1966 a Ford Foundation grant for three months of travel and study in England and Israel to investigate their cooperative economic systems.

On her return to Mississippi, she found that Head Start had finally been refunded. It was a constant struggle. Every few months, delegations had to travel to Washington to put forward the need for the continuation of the programs. Not only were thousands of children getting a decent start in life, but an investment in children, Marian knew, would cut down on future government expenses.

More and more she was pointing her finger at the federal government and finding it lax in implementing its own laws. For example, in the matter of education she found that the federal government was letting white school boards determine the pace of integration, which was moving slowly. These same school boards sat idly by when white teachers hassled African-American children who had the courage to enter white schools, and they approved of white parents setting up private schools to avoid integration. The government, Marian charged, was also doing little to enforce the Voting Rights Act or to protect people against the continuing violence.

Her voice calling for change was strong, persistent, and determined, and it was heard in the nation's capital. In March 1967, Marian testified in Washington, D.C., before the Senate Subcommittee on Employment, Manpower, and Poverty. The committee chair was Senator Joseph Clark of Pennsylvania. Serving with him were Senators Jacob Javits and Robert Kennedy of New York and Senator George Murphy of California.

The committee members listened attentively to the bright young woman only 27 years of age. Clear-voiced, confident, and eloquent, Marian Wright brought to life the economic changes in the Delta and the widespread unemployment. Facts and figures at her fingertips, she described the mechanization of cotton farming and what it meant. Jobs that black tenant farmers and sharecroppers relied on—such as breaking up the soil, planting, and harvesting—were now done by machines. Many had fled north in search of work but tens of thousands could not afford the fare for such a change.

In addition, she pointed out, the federal subsidy program had also reduced the number of jobs. The program worked this way: Senator Eastland, for example, was paid more than $160,000 in 1967 in subsidies to produce less cotton. For farm workers, it meant fewer jobs because of the cutback in the number of acres on which cotton was growing. Yet the poor families who had worked the land received no part of the subsidy.

She added more facts: the minimum wage of $1.00 per hour meant it was cheaper to use chemical sprays to kill weeds than to employ labor, and the government introduction of food stamps on which poor families depended had eliminated the distribution of free surplus food. But people were required to pay for food stamps and they had no money for that, even at $2.00 a person.

At the end of her testimony, Marian urged the committee members to visit the South—to visit Mississippi—and to see for themselves the conditions of hunger and starvation. She hoped to show them tenant farmers who literally had no food to eat in "this rich American country."

Persuaded by Marian's arguments, the Senate subcommittee sent an advance team to Jackson to make plans for holding hearings there. On the team was Peter Edelman, Senator Kennedy's legislative assistant, who got in touch with Marian to discuss the situation with her.

When the hearings opened in Jackson in April 1967, the four senators—Clark, Kennedy, Javits, and Murphy—arrived with members of their investigative teams. As she had during the hearings in Washington, Marian again testified. She was blunt, clear, and compassionate about the people she described. "They're starving and those who can get the bus fare to go North are going North. But there is absolutely nothing for them to do. There is nowhere to go, and somebody must begin to respond to them. . . . Starvation," she said, "is a major, major problem, now."

Also testifying was Mrs. Fannie Lou Hamer. The youngest of 20 children of a sharecropper's family, she talked from personal experience. She also reported about the advantages of the Head Start program, urging its continued refunding. The program was important, she said, because it gave adults as well as children "a head start."

When the hearings were over, Marian suggested that the senators see for themselves "the empty cupboards in the Delta" and parents begging for food to feed their children. Senators Javits and Murphy returned to Washington but Senators Kennedy and Clark stayed. Marian, acting as their guide, led the two senators from house to house. At one small dark shanty in the rural town of Cleveland, Mrs. Annie White was busy washing the family's clothes in a metal tub while her children sat on the dirt floor around her. Senator Kennedy stooped down and tried to get a two-year-old girl to respond to his playfulness—touching her hand and smiling—only to see the child, her stomach bloated from malnutrition, sit quietly, passive, listless, and unresponsive. Marian, observing the scene, was moved to "near tears," she would later say. And Senator Kennedy won her deepest respect and affection for his emotional reaction to the desolate household.

Marian took Senators Kennedy and Clark and their aides to other shacks, all of which showed a level of poverty they had not known existed—poverty that was hidden away. Peter Edelman, there with Senator Kennedy, would comment at a later date, "What's burned in my mind is seeing children in the United States of America who had bloated bellies and who had sores that wouldn't heal. That's what was shocking about Mississippi in 1967."

Marian's persistence in publicizing the unrelieved hunger in Mississippi brought it to national attention and won at least one immediate change. The senators, on their return to Washington, persuaded Secretary of Agriculture Orville Freeman to make food stamps free.

Poverty in the United States in the mid-1960s had become a critical issue arousing many organizations to action. Among them was the Field Foundation. The director, Leslie W. Dunbar, had met and become a friend of Marian during frequent visits to Mississippi. A supporter of the voter education projects and the Head Start programs, Dunbar knew firsthand the poverty of southern black people. On his recommendation, the Field

Senator Robert Kennedy, with Marian Wright and an aide (at left),
visiting a home in the Delta

Foundation underwrote a medical project to study health conditions in Mississippi.

The results of the study made headlines in the *New York Times* on June 17, 1967. Nan Robertson, in an article titled SEVERE HUNGER FOUND IN MISSISSIPPI, reported on the project and its findings. "Pitiful," "alarming," "unbelievable," "appalling," were the strong words used by the medical team. The report accused many local doctors of barely examining poor children and of showing no compassion toward those they treated.

The investigating team made it clear, moreover, that the boys and girls they saw "were hungry . . . weak, in pain, sick; their lives are being shortened. . . . They are suffering from hunger and disease directly or indirectly they are dying from them . . . which is exactly what 'starvation' means."

Committee expert Dr. Joseph Brenner from the medical department of the Massachusetts Institute of Technology said, "It is fantastic that this should be so in the wealthiest nation in the world . . . the wealthiest nation that ever was."

In 1967, the infant mortality rate in Mississippi was the highest in the nation, and conditions for African Americans generally were getting worse.

Senate hearings and various reports and inquiries made increasingly clear the scope of poverty within the nation. It had ravaged Indian reservations, mining towns, city ghettoes, rural areas, and migrant workers' camps. After years of urban unrest, the anger and rage of the poor finally exploded in the summer of 1967. Riots—some called them rebellions—tore apart 100 cities. People were tired of neglect and injustice in every phase of their lives—in jobs, housing, on the police force, and in the courts. Newark, New Jersey, broke into flames in July. In August, riots and arson in Detroit, Michigan, almost destroyed the city. Eighty people died in the conflagrations and the violence.

Riots are the language of the poor, said Martin Luther King, Jr., and by the end of 1967 he began to see that poverty-stricken conditions were no longer receiving national attention. A new crisis—the war in Vietnam— was claiming the front pages of the newspapers.

By 1967, the war had expanded and Dr. King recognized at once the connection between the monetary needs of the war and the neglect of the poor. Poverty at home and the war overseas were inseparable, he said. It cost, he explained, $50,000 for each enemy we killed in Vietnam, but we spent only $53 for each person classified as poor at home. In 1967, one in every seven was living below the poverty line. In the South, where the face of poverty was everywhere, field hands were earning as little as $3.00 a day.

"The promises of the Great Society have been shot down on the battlefields of Vietnam," he said, "making the poor—black and white—bear the burdens of the war."

Poverty in the United States brought Marian Wright and Martin Luther King, Jr., together again. They joined forces to keep national attention focused on the poor.

CHAPTER TEN

The Poor People's Campaign

MARIAN AND DR. KING HAD KNOWN EACH OTHER IN Atlanta when she was a student at Spelman. She, the daughter of a Baptist minister, and he, the copastor with his father of Atlanta's great Ebenezer Baptist Church, had become friends.

By 1967, the civil rights movement was changing course. New organizations were leading African Americans to explore bolder and more aggressive tactics for winning their economic and political rights. Appealing in particular to young urban people was the Black Panther party, a group of militants who rejected Dr. King's philosophy of non-violent resistance. The Panthers had grown popular not only through radical confrontations with the white power structure, but through the success of their programs of free breakfasts and remedial schools. By 1968, the Black Panthers had chapters in 25 cities. The leaders, Stokely Carmichael and Huey Newton, were charismatic power figures and popular with the media.

While a segment of the movement was growing more radical and

The Reverend Martin Luther King, Jr.

defiant, Dr. King, still urging non-violent resistance, was trying to maintain his leadership as the national spokesperson for the country's African-American population. He needed an important issue and Marian Wright helped Dr. King address the question of hunger in the United States and develop it into a major crusade. Not only had the promise of the Great Society not been met, but conditions had worsened.

The question of poverty and hunger was very much on Marian's mind in 1967, and she had the occasion to discuss the subject with Senator Kennedy with whom she had become friendly following his visit to the Mississippi Delta. In August, she and Peter Edelman stopped off to see the senator in his Hickory Hill home in Virginia. As usual, when they met they talked about the conditions of the poor and their frustration that the government, and the Department of Agriculture in particular, was doing nothing to feed the hungry. When Marian mentioned that she planned to see Martin Luther King, Jr., in Atlanta, Kennedy remarked, "Tell him to bring the poor people to Washington." It would be a way to make them visible.

Marian brought the suggestion to Dr. King and, she would remember he "instinctively felt that [the suggestion] was right and treated me as if

I was an emissary of grace. . . . Out of that the Poor People's Campaign was born."

Dr. King saw in the idea a way to dramatize the whole issue of poverty. He envisioned a march that would bring to the nation's capital a non-violent and multi-racial army of the poor from all parts of the country, demanding an income or jobs. A massive turnout would grip the people's imaginations and focus attention on the desperate conditions of millions in affluent America.

Not everyone on Dr. King's staff shared his enthusiasm. Many thought it was not the time to bring the poor to Washington.

The idea was discussed further at a five-day Southern Christian Leadership Conference retreat in Warrenton, Virginia. Marian, at the SCLC retreat, supported Dr. King: the march would alert the public to the misery she witnessed daily in Mississippi. She suggested, according to author David Garrow in his book *Bearing the Cross,* "a fast and sit-in at the office of the U.S. Labor Secretary W. Willard Wirtz." She proposed the idea "that a group of religious and labor leaders with Dr. King and a half-a-dozen poor folks would go to Wirtz's office and sit-in and just say they were going to stay there and fast or be jailed or whatever it was until they provided jobs."

Dr. King was deeply concerned in 1967 by the explosions of violence in large cities and the terrible unrest. He realized that African Americans had won the right to vote but they had not gained jobs, equal justice in the courts of law nor better housing, education, and medical care. The persistent lack of equality made him question basic social values. Perhaps the form of society itself had to change to meet the needs of people for it to become person-oriented rather than profit-oriented. The march on Washington seemed to Dr. King, and to Marian, a course of action that would move the process forward and force the country to focus on the social needs of the tens of thousands of poor people who would be camped on the streets of Washington, D.C.

Dr. King's high hopes notwithstanding, the campaign did not excite attention. By 1968, the Vietnam War was getting top billing. The U.S. poor could not compete with the drama of war events, of death and destruction, shown daily on television. Nor could they compete with a growing anti-war movement. Heightening tensions was the Vietnam Tet offensive in 1968. The shattering U.S. defeat increased the toll of dead soldiers and aroused greater opposition to the war. For an increasing number of U. S. citizens and members of Congress, nothing seemed to matter but ending the war and bringing the soldiers home.

As if the Tet offensive was not crippling enough to the United States government, on March 1, the President's Commission on Civil Disobedience issued its findings. The commission, appointed after the 1967 urban violence, found "white racism chiefly to blame for the explosive conditions that sparked the riots in American cities." And, said the report, "Discrimination and segregation have long permeated much of American life; they now threaten the future of every American." What was needed, said the commission, was "sustained, compassionate, massive action backed by the resources of the most powerful and richest nation on this earth. . . ." It will "require new attitudes, new understanding, and above all new will." To improve conditions within urban centers the report recommended, among other things, the immediate creation of two million jobs, job training, and housing for low and moderate income people.

But government leaders were not listening to the report. They concentrated on events abroad, diverting moneys from peoples' programs to make up the billions of dollars needed for the war. The report, however, supported Martin Luther King, Jr., and Marian Wright in their decision to focus attention on those persistently left out of the American dream.

Events in the critical year of 1968 continued on a dramatic sweep. President Johnson's popularity plummeted, reaching a new low in March. His failure was brought on by poverty at home, a powerful anti-war movement, and the divisiveness of the Vietnam War. To complicate matters, Robert Kennedy declared his race for the presidency. On the last day of March, President Johnson stunned the nation by announcing that he would not seek re-election.

That same evening Martin Luther King, Jr., spoke at the Washington Cathedral on his favorite theme—his plan to bring poor people to Washington. Unrelenting in his criticism of President Johnson, he again tied the nation's poverty to the Vietnam War.

Throughout March, the SCLC staff worried about the lack of enthusiasm for the Poor People's Campaign. But Dr. King had set his mind on it. This would be a crucial fight, a last crusade to try to change social conditions through non-violent means. To whip up support, Dr. King and two aides traveled in a small chartered plane, and his staff in cars, to towns and cities in the South to confer with black leaders. He described to them his vision of the crusade: It would start in the shacks of Mississippi, Alabama, and Georgia, and in the city slums of Chicago and Detroit, and move to a shantytown "tent-in" on the mall in Washington, D.C., between the Lincoln Memorial and the Washington monument.

Throughout the early months of 1968, Marian, still in Jackson, was part of the legislative planning for the march. At the same time she was following her own agenda. It was time to move on, to relocate to Washington, D.C., the seat of power.

She had made countless trips to Washington to fight for refunding for Head Start. Her commitment to the children and to the poor could be better served if she were close to Congress and the White House. As an advocate for the poor, perhaps she could influence the direction of federal programs on their behalf. An added inducement was her growing friendship with Kennedy aide Peter Edelman, who worked in Washington.

Her relocation was helped along by a 1968 grant from the Field Foundation. It provided funds for a series of studies she wanted to undertake called the Washington Research Project, which would investigate the laws passed on behalf of the poor and minorities to be sure that these laws were really benefiting them.

While Marian was doing the difficult and tedious chores of making a major change after four years in Mississippi, Martin Luther King, Jr., was on a continuous campaign to bring the poor to Washington. He was under great emotional strain, said his biographer David Garrow, from a ceaseless round of meetings and talks. He was also discouraged by the lack of excitement about his poor people's crusade.

On April 3, Dr. King was in Memphis, Tennessee, in support of the striking sanitation workers. He lodged at the Lorraine Motel with members of his staff, among them Ralph Abernathy, Andrew Young, and Jesse Jackson. The next evening, April 4, King and his aides were preparing to attend a dinner at a friend's home. While he was standing on a balcony of the motel shots rang out. A bullet hit Dr. King. He died one hour later.

The assassination of Dr. Martin Luther King, Jr., released torrents of rage. Tides of violence swept through city after city. The nation's capital was scorched by fires. The shock almost paralyzed the leadership of King's organization, the SCLC. They could not deal with the work facing them and did not know how to proceed with the Poor People's Campaign. But they committed themselves to carry out Dr. King's wishes, to carry out his mission. It was important that his work go forward. To help them with the legislative work they asked Marian Wright to give additional time to the campaign. Though profoundly shocked by the murder of Dr. King and the loss of a friend, she agreed to coordinate the campaign and to serve as the congressional and federal agency liaison.

Assisting Marian were Peter Edelman, counsel Bill Smith of the poverty subcommittee, and several officials in the Johnson administration. In addition to proposing new legislation to increase jobs and housing, Marian and her committee were busy day and night drawing up a practical program to make the social legislation already enacted effective. For example, they asked the Department of Justice to fully enforce the civil rights laws. They also requested the proper agency to accord welfare recipients their full rights; and they urged Johnson's Office of Economic Opportunity to see to it that the poor participated in programs related to them. For the benefit and care of children, they requested that the nation's poor children be served free lunches. They also urged the Department of Agriculture to carry out the reforms already placed before it and to provide the nation's 1,000 poorest communities with a food program.

The proposals written up, the Reverend Abernathy, who had become the head of SCLC, launched the Poor People's Campaign in Washington on April 29. He led a hundred-member delegation of the poor and church and labor leaders to lobby Congress.

Though the group was disorganized, appearing late for appointments, the people voiced their pleas dramatically when they described their hard lives and a future filled with despair. In the lobby of the Department of Agriculture, Abernathy was eloquent. He invoked the assassination of Dr. King and commented that Dr. King's work would continue and that they were in Washington to carry his dream forward.

In mid-May contingents of the poor began arriving in Washington. They came on foot, in cars and trucks, in old buses, and in mule-driven carts. They came from the shanties of Appalachia, from Indian reservations, and from Mississippi where Mrs. Fannie Lou Hamer spoke to them

Mule train arriving in Washington, D.C., for Poor People's Campaign

in the Delta town of Marks where the mule train was starting out. They came from the city streets of New York, Boston, Chicago, and Los Angeles. They demanded *ACTION NOW*. Religious and labor groups came— everyone full of pride; eager, excited, and hopeful that their voices would reach the government.

Awaiting the crusaders was a settlement christened Resurrection City by Dr. Abernathy. Woodsheds and tents to house 3,000 were built on the park land south of the Reflecting Pool. The overflow crowd settled in Lafayette Square on Pennsylvania Avenue across from the White House. Schools were set up for youngsters; medical teams took care of the sick; and writers and teachers came to hold class and talk.

Resurrection City, Poor People's Campaign

Coretta Scott King arrived on May 12 accompanied by her four children. Six weeks after Dr. King's murder she came to lead the welfare mothers in their march scheduled for the afternoon. On hand to greet her was Ethel Kennedy, wife of Senator Robert Kennedy, and other luminaries.

After a few days, it began to rain. It rained for a full month from mid-May to mid-June turning Resurrection City into a mess of mud and puddles. The press began to write about the problems at the encampment, not the problems of the poor. Before the campaign could make itself heard, the press was calling it a failure.

Years later Marian Wright would recall how difficult it was to carry on the struggle. Hurt and grieving over the loss of Dr. King, she like others felt the need to implement his work. She remembered the rain and the mud and rushing between Resurrection City and the Pitts Motel where the SCLC staff was staying. She recalled how hard it was to get to people and to make them understand why she wanted them to be witnesses at government agencies.

She succeeded in getting 15 people together and helping them formulate their stories so that government officials would hear what they were saying. At the new Senate office building each one gave a sad account of what happened to them because of the lack of money.

Mrs. Tina Kruger described how a couple of migrant parents had handed her a starving infant and said, "Here, you take this baby home because I have nothing to feed him. He is dying of starvation, and I do not want him to die in my home."

Mrs. Ellis Blackhorse, a Native American from South Dakota, explained to the senators that she was a diabetic and could not live on the starchy food she was given and she had no money to buy other food.

A high school student explained she had dropped out of school because

Puddles and mud in Resurrection City

she could not stand handing in a card to pay for her lunch. Her card was a different color from the other cards. "You feel low," she said. "We should not have certain colors to separate us: like one rich, one poor. . . ."

No one really listened.

On June 6, in the midst of this heartbreaking campaign that could not pull itself together, Marian celebrated her 29th birthday. June 6 was also the day on which Senator Robert Kennedy was assassinated. The deaths of two leaders allied to the struggles of poor people brought despair and hopelessness. Those who had remained frozen at King's death finally let themselves grieve when the Kennedy funeral procession stopped at Resurrection City in homage to Dr. King and to the poor. The hearse was in front of the Lincoln Memorial when people began to sing the "Battle Hymn of the Republic." It was a profound moment of mourning, for not only were the thousands grieving over Robert Kennedy but once again over the loss of their leader, Martin Luther King, Jr.

Dr. Abernathy quietly led a delegation to the Kennedy funeral at Arlington National Cemetery and then back across Memorial Bridge to Resurrection City.

To bolster the remnants of the Poor People's Campaign, 100,000 people descended on Washington on June 19 for Solidarity Day. They came from all parts of the country to offer support, but by then the city police had notified the encampment officials that Resurrection City had to be closed down.

June 24 was the city's last day. Many stood around with their few possessions; they had no place to go. Their hopes for attention had withered early on. After the first few days the compassion in the nation's capital had turned to annoyance at the ragged army that had littered the streets.

Still, there were some small successes. Changes were made in the food program when Secretary of Agriculture Orville Freeman urged Congress to add $300 to $400 million to the 1969 budget for the next 12 months. "This will not end hunger in the United States, but it will make a big down payment on a program to end hunger shortly," he said.

Though many saw a major defeat in the collapse of Resurrection City, Marian Wright sounded a different voice. She had enormous resilience. Friends always talked about her strength and good spirits. Behind her were the experiences of her upbringing when the imagination and initiative of her parents turned what could have been a calamity into a good. A milestone in her recollections had to be the time her father built a playground for his community so that young African-American children would not feel the pain of exclusion from the town's segregated playground. Or how her parents protected the elderly and the helpless. The struggle always went on. So now on this occasion, she said Resurrection City did not mean the end of the struggle. "I don't think anybody ever has a right to give up on children or give up on the poor. The needs remain. The needs grow," she would say.

Even the terrible loss of Dr. King should not slow the momentum of moving forward. "None of us," she said, "had his eloquence and certainly not his goodness, but in our own ways, with our hands and our limited visions, we can try and craft together his dream."

Like her parents, Marian, in her own way, would try to build a "playground" for those left out of the magic circle. The end of Resurrection City was "a time to regroup, rethink, and build new paths to the future, to rethink the country's problems of poverty and race." The Poor People's Campaign was a battle on a long road.

CHAPTER ELEVEN

New Paths

MARIAN HAD ALWAYS NEGLECTED HER PERSONAL LIFE because urgent problems claimed her. But during late 1967 and early 1968, throughout the weeks of the terrible murders of King and Kennedy, and the turmoil of the Poor People's Campaign, she had the encouragement and support of a friend she had made in Mississippi. She would later say that she and Peter Edelman fell in love "over hungry children."

Edelman first came to Mississippi as a Kennedy aide to prepare for the Senate subcommittee hearings into poverty. He looked up Marian Wright, who had testified on the subject in Washington, D.C. On his subsequent visits to Mississippi or when she traveled to Washington, they would get together. Their talk moved from children and hunger to personal interest in each other. Edelman saw in Marian "a real grace . . . a beautiful laugh" and "particularly delicate" hands. Marian saw in Peter a man who would let her lead her own life.

He was 30, a year older than Marian, and a rather gentle young man.

Raised in Minneapolis, Minnesota, and a graduate of Harvard University and Harvard Law School, he had spent years in government service. After clerking in 1962 for Supreme Court Justice Arthur Goldberg, he joined the Department of Justice legal staff. In 1964, he began working for the Kennedy campaign and became one of the senator's legislative assistants.

It did not seem to matter to the two young people in love that they were of different religions and races. She, a Baptist African American, and he, Jewish and white, had more in common than separated them. They came from families that stressed the importance of education. Both of them, sensitive and compassionate, shunned the high-salaried jobs in private or corporate law to which their Ivy League educations gave them easy access. In their moral and social codes, everyone deserved a fair deal, and government had to be responsive to the needs of the poor and the unemployed.

They made a good team. She was connected to the civil rights struggles and its leadership and he knew his way around official Washington, whom to see in government and how to get there. She was an activist, a doer; he more the scholar and teacher.

On July 14 in the summer of 1968, Marian and Peter were married. The social event took place at the home of Peter's friend Adam Walinsky, who had also been a Kennedy legislative assistant. Two hundred friends and family members gathered in Walinsky's large garden on a beautiful sunny afternoon. The bride, dressed in white, wore a tiara of small white rosebuds and carried a bouquet of white rosebuds adorned with streaming ribbons. The groom wore a white silk Nehru jacket over dark pants and a turtleneck sweater. Wreathed in smiles, they stood before Marian's friend, the Reverend William Sloane Coffin, Jr., who officiated at a simple 15-minute ceremony. Also present was Arthur J. Goldberg, who told the couple, whose "lives had been so intimately touched with tragedies

Marian Wright and Peter Edelman on their wedding day,
with the Reverend William Sloane Coffin in background

that shook a nation," that "it was not easy in such a year as this to celebrate an event of joy."

But joyful it was. Marian's mother, Mrs. Wright, and members of her
large southern family met and mixed with Peter's midwestern family and
many highly placed government officials and civil rights leaders.

Peter Edelman was among the Kennedy aides who had received a Ford
Foundation grant to ease the transition from public life into other careers.
The newlyweds used the grant to take a trip around the world visiting

Europe, East Africa, India, Southeast Asia and Japan. In some cities, Peter gave lectures while Marian observed the urban poverty.

On their return to Washington five months later, and after settling into their new home, Peter Edelman became the associate director of the Robert Kennedy Memorial, and Marian resumed her work as director of the Washington Research Project.

Working in coalition with other organizations, she and her small staff undertook an intensive study of education for the poor. Specifically they investigated "Title I," a government program that had allocated more than a billion dollars to the education of poor children. Through audits of accounts and careful research, Marian discovered that the funds did not reach poor children in the way the act provided. Instead her study showed that money was being spent on programs that barely helped poor kids or did not help them at all. In many instances, money did not go to the poorest school districts, but to those already well funded.

It seemed to Marian a significant piece of investigative work, confirming the continued neglect of poor children. When the capital's leading newspaper, the *Washington Post*, gave her study front-page coverage, it encouraged her to expect the government to make significant changes. At least it would investigate the charges! Nothing happened. Everything went on as usual; poor children remained neglected.

She remarked that she "still had the illusion that if you tell people the truth they will do the right thing." She called it her first big political lesson in Washington. Like many others before her, she had to learn that it took much more than telling the truth to change conditions. It was a long struggle.

She soon learned another political lesson in Washington. She found that she could not appear before a government agency with a significant request unless she had support behind her. Who was she? For whom did she speak? "Who are your troops?" Congressman John Brademas of the House Education and Labor Committee asked her when she appeared before him to request that he oppose a bill that would turn Head Start over to the states. She knew what would happen in Mississippi where the state government did not want the program.

Based on her increasing knowledge of the legislative process, Marian carefully planned the procedures for being heard by Congress; procedures that would make government undertake responsibility for the care and education of children.

To gain support for a new proposal, she organized a broad coalition of church, education and labor groups, welfare mothers, feminists, and others. Together they drafted the child development bill of 1971. It would increase aid for preschool children and protect and extend Head Start. As a result of hard work and persuasive and careful lobbying, Congress passed the bill. The coalition of organizations was jubilant that it had won a tremendous victory: The government would finally take responsibility for the country's children. The celebrations were premature, however. Unexpectedly President Nixon vetoed the bill, claiming that it weakened the family. The failure of the bill to win presidential approval "shattered" Marian. She had never considered the possibility of a veto!

She did not give up, however, and presented the bill a year later. By then conservatives had broadened their opposition and the bill never became law. Again, she called it a learning experience.

Marian was busy as well with her own growing family. Joshua was born in August 1969, and Jonah in October 1970. In 1971, the family of four moved to Boston where Peter became vice president of the University of Massachusetts and Marian accepted a position as director of the Harvard University Center for Law and Education. Once each week she flew to

Washington to oversee the Washington Research Project. That year, 1971, *Time* magazine named her one of the country's 200 young leaders.

No matter where she was or what she was doing, the idea of working to protect children had become central to her thinking: to give all children, regardless of class or race, a decent start in life and to assure for them a healthy, productive future.

CHAPTER TWELVE

The 101st Senator

$\mathcal{E}$VERYONE BETWEEN BIRTH AND 18 YEARS OF AGE IS considered a child. Of the total United States population of 260 million, there are 68 million children. Among them are 15 million living in poverty, according to 1993 statistics—an increase of five million since 1973. "Living in poverty" is defined as families of four whose incomes are less than $14,763 a year—the amount of money judged essential for food, shelter, and clothing. And it means that one child in approximately every five is deprived of basic necessities.

Children trapped by poverty can be found everywhere but especially in homeless shelters, welfare hotels, crowded housing projects, as well as in rural areas, cities, and suburbs. They are children of black and Latino minorities and they are white children. In fact, "the majority of poor children are white, not black . . . the majority of the poor are in rural and suburban areas and not in the inner cities," Marian Wright Edelman told an interviewer for *Black Enterprise* magazine. What was true, she continued, was that a disproportionate number of black and minority children suffer from poverty and its disastrous effects.

The road to Marian Wright Edelman's concern for poor children started in rural Mississippi in 1965, at about the time she saw the benefits of the Head Start programs for both children and their parents. She had her first skirmishes with the United States government to get the programs refunded. By 1967, she had become a spokesperson for Mississippi's poor, eloquently testifying on their behalf before Senate subcommittees. In 1968, she was a moving spirit behind the Poor People's Campaign. And from 1968 to 1973, as head of the Washington Research Project, she tried to make the laws protecting poor people effective.

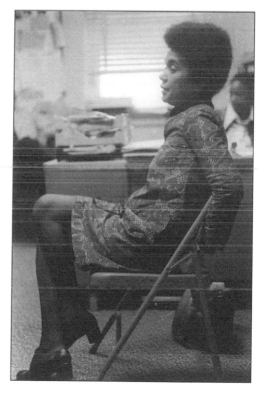

Marian in the late 1960s and early 1970s

By 1973, her work on behalf of children came together into a leaner and sharper focus. Clearly, the problems of the poor and solutions to the problems were complex. New strategies were needed to leap over the barriers of worn out policies, to cut through the red tape that blocked solutions, to educate the American people in the perils of poverty, and to convince the government to invest in poor people because poverty endangered its leadership in the global economy.

To do the kind of job Edelman now saw as crucial would require an effective new organization, a showcase of knowledge and skills, and in 1973, she received grants to found the Children's Defense Fund. For a few years—until 1977—the fledgling group functioned as a component of the Washington Research Project, Inc. Its first publication was "Children Out of School in America."

From the beginning her constituency was the nation's poor children, the millions she saw as voiceless and powerless; "the silent majority," she called them. And among those millions she dedicated herself to helping "those who have the least."

A ringing reminder of the poor's despair was in the voice of a young man in Jackson, Mississippi, after the murder of Martin Luther King, Jr., in 1968. Marian was urging a group of youngsters to avoid violence, warning that violence would be harmful to their futures. One angry young boy turned to her and said, "Lady, why should I listen to you? Lady, I ain't got no future."

Through children living in poverty, she could show the devastating effects of hunger and poor health. She could highlight how these conditions led to social ills. She could also track exactly how money invested in early childhood cut down government expenses in later life.

Though at first it was Edelman's idea to highlight the violence of poverty through children, before long her commitment to children themselves became personal and passionate. If she could, she would know each one by name.

In the summer of 1973, she launched her new organization from rooms she found in an old Victorian house in Cambridge, Massachusetts. From the beginning she conceived of the organization as non-profit and national in scope. Its mission would be to "provide systematic and long-term assistance to children and to make their needs an important matter of public policy." She adapted an old fisherman's prayer into a logo for the new organization:

> Dear Lord
>
> Be good to me
>
> The sea is so wide
>
> and my boat is so small.

Logo of the newly formed Children's Defense Fund

The drawing for the logo was made by a small child.

In her book *Families in Peril*, she wrote that the Children's Defense Fund "came into existence . . . because we recognized that support for whatever was labeled black and poor was shrinking and that new ways had to be found to articulate and respond to the continuing problems of poverty and race, ways that appealed to the self-interest as well as the conscience of the American people."

Funds for the Children's Defense Fund would come from foundations, corporate businesses, and the public. To depend on government funds, she said, would make it difficult for her to influence or to be critical of government. By accepting funds from the public and private sectors, however, she could involve the whole community and, she said, it "takes a whole community to raise a kid."

In a continuously creative process, CDF focused on all children—black and white, poor and rich—and on the wide range of problems they face from poverty to teenage pregnancy. The emphasis would always be on those most in need and least protected: kids who were disabled, drug-addicted, or AIDS-infected; the homeless; the school dropouts; and children whose own parents often found them too difficult to care for and whom others did not care about.

The organization came into being toward the end of Richard Nixon's presidency, 1966–1974. Though they were conservative years, the government did increase funds for food programs and Head Start. Still, they were not the best years to try to influence legislation on behalf of the poor. Nor were the following years under Presidents Ford and Carter much better for child welfare programs. Nevertheless, through the work of CDF and other child advocacy groups, the plight of children was kept before the public.

Taking a leadership role, CDF in 1977 helped a coalition of organizations representing the handicapped win a major victory. The guiding star for the militant campaign was Daniel Yohalem, head of CDF's legal division. But the strength and unity were provided by the handicapped themselves who staged sit-ins at the Washington, D.C., office of Joseph A. Califano, Secretary of Health, Education and Welfare. Similar demonstrations were held at 10 regional offices throughout the country.

The handicapped were demanding that Califano approve new regulations that would implement a 1973 law prohibiting discrimination by recipients of public funds. The new rules would finally give the disabled equal rights in employment, education, and all health and welfare programs. For example, one million disabled children would be permitted to enter public schools from which they had been barred.

It took weeks of militant demonstrations by the handicapped, who staged protests not only at Califano's office but also in front of his home and at meetings where he spoke. In San Francisco the demonstrators had the support of local unions and civil rights groups.

The ultimate signing of the regulations by Califano ushered in a new era for the handicapped. And the militant activities led by CDF placed it in the forefront of organizations fighting for the protection of those who had no voice and no access to power.

In 1979, Marian and her family moved back to Washington, D.C., where Peter Edelman became a professor of law at Georgetown University. By now, there were three young sons in the family. Ezra was born in Boston in 1974. From the time of first-born son Joshua's early childhood, the

Marian at the beach with her three young sons,
Ezra on her lap, Jonah, and Joshua

Marian Wright Edelman and Peter Edelman in their home in the mid-1980s

Edelmans had help in the home. Marian's mother had recommended a Bennettsville neighbor and friend. Mrs. Amy Byers became part of the Edelman household and a surrogate grandmother. Also around the family's home in northwest Washington was a community of neighbors providing a safe haven. The home care and the friendly community made it possible for both Marian and Peter Edelman to pursue full-time careers.

In 1980, Ronald Reagan was elected to the presidency. A landslide victory enabled him to put into immediate effect his conservative policies. The gains that Marian Wright Edelman, CDF, and other organizations had brought about were soon cut back. Reagan dismantled welfare programs that had been built up over the previous 20 years. These benefits caused a sluggish economy and only increased the problems they were supposed to solve, he said.

After two years in office, Reagan's deep reductions in benefits for low-income families and children went into effect. In fiscal year 1982, Congress cut $35 billion in domestic programs, including $10 billion in programs for children. The tide swept over everything: Medicaid, food stamps, school lunches and breakfasts that were often the only meals poor kids had, child health such as immunization, day care services that enabled poor mothers to work, public housing, and education. The results of the reductions were immediate and disastrous, adding millions of children to the poverty rolls.

Congress was the battling ground, an arena for the defense of and opposition to the cuts. And Marian Wright Edelman had become an awesome figure on Capitol Hill, an outstanding lobbyist. Always a watchful eye over the country's poor children, she showed up in congressional offices armed with the most recent data to raise her voice against the destruction of children's programs. In rapid-fire talk, persistent, and tireless, she argued her case. Senator Edward Kennedy dubbed her "the 101st senator on children's issues."

"I can be as tough as nails, just as anybody who believes in anything has to be tough as nails," she would remark on a CBS "60 Minutes" interview. Elaborating further, she commented, "I have no objection to twisting arms for kids. I have no objection to doing anything that the law permits me to do for kids."

"You have to watch every minute," was the way she put it. "Changing social policy is just dogged hard work and persistence. There's no great magic about it. You have to stay on people and make it easier for them to do what you want them to do than not to do it. So we're good pests. I'm a good pest is what I am."

Marian Wright Edelman in her office, at a Children's Defense Fund conference, and at "A Celebration of Children" at the Washington Cathedral

She was more than "a good pest." She was stinging, blunt, and unrelenting in notifying Congress and the country in the mid-1980s that "poverty is the greatest child killer in the affluent United States." Elaborating further she said, "More American children die each year from poverty than from traffic fatalities and suicide combined. . . . Yet our national leaders have invested $3.5 billion in research for a new 'Star Wars' system to make our defenses impenetrable against every missile in space, while thousands of American infants are dying in our cities and rural areas from preventable infant mortality."

While these cuts were assaulting benefit programs, Edelman and her staff were busy working on a study called Black and White Children in America. In the course of their work, they began to focus on the social problem of teenage pregnancy. In 1983, teenage pregnancy had developed into a major issue, with one out of ten teenagers becoming pregnant. Most of them were not married when they gave birth, and this situation existed in both white and black families.

Not only did these youngsters drop out of school, but they were unemployed and had no source of income. Most of them went on welfare, had little if any prenatal care, and had no idea how to care for an infant. This new turn in the teenage culture not only harmed the youngsters but required millions of dollars for their care.

To address the problem, Edelman and CDF launched a major campaign. Posters, radio and television announcements, newspaper stories, public talks at schools and churches, and imaginative programs such as the Adolescent Pregnancy Prevention Clearinghouse alerted the public to a major social problem. The programs dealt with prevention by providing youngsters with different options for their future. Schools were prodded to create innovative programs that would keep teenagers in school and build up their self-esteem so that they would not drift into the self-destructive behavior of early pregnancy.

The reductions in social benefits brought a new symptom of the times. Homeless men and women with their children were crowding into shelters or sleeping in cars and on the streets. The poor were making themselves visible. It was impossible to turn away or to deny the shame of such poverty on the cities' rich streets.

During the early Reagan years, CDF decided it would be best to hold on to laws already in place rather than to expand or change them. But by the mid-1980s the cutbacks were being reversed under the combined pressures on Congress by CDF, the labor movement, parents' organizations, and many other advocacy groups. In 1984, Medicaid coverage was expanded to cover expectant mothers, and in 1987 the Reagan administration was forced to add a $500 million increase to its $36 billion budget for families and children's health and education needs.

By the mid-1980s, Marian Wright Edelman herself had become a prominent national figure. Honors had come her way in the 1960s and 1970s and in 1983 the *Ladies Home Journal* named her one of the 100 most influential women in America. In 1985, she won a MacArthur Foundation Prize Fellowship, and in 1986 Harvard University invited her to deliver the W. E. B. DuBois lectures, a distinguished appointment. The lectures were published a year later by Harvard University Press under the title *Families in Peril: An Agenda for Social Change*.

In the book, as in the lectures, Edelman found children all over the world in peril. In a single day, she pointed out, 40,000 children in the world die from malnutrition and infections. These children were dying, she said, while billions of dollars were spent on military weapons.

Led by our own country, the nations of the world spent $2.7 billion each day on "weapons of death that are of no use to the hungry and sick children of the world." The arms race, she said, robs the world's children of their future and steals the present, plunging them into a life of "relentless poverty and the hunger and disease it breeds."

Talking about the United States, she pointed out that the poorest Americans are children. Economic and social barriers "cripple millions of children and families and rob America of vitally needed human resources for the 21st century." In 1987, statistics showed an increase to 33 million now poor, among them 13 million children. It was a black and white crisis, not only a black crisis. Nearly one half of black children were poor, and one sixth of white children were in the same category.

Marian Wright Edelman not only lectured at Harvard, she was in demand as a speaker at meetings and conferences. Traveling across the country, she observed that the public was more receptive to what she was saying. The Reagan years were coming to an end, and presidential elections would be held in 1988. Contenders George Bush and Michael Dukakis promised change. "The year of the child" was declared in 1988 and both candidates spoke of increasing day care for working mothers. The times seemed favorable for more aggressive actions—to again mount a campaign for government legislation on behalf of children.

CHAPTER THIRTEEN

The Battle for Child Care

*M*ARIAN WRIGHT EDELMAN ALWAYS DID MORE HOME-work than she had to, and learning every detail, every shade of the ins-and-outs of the congressional legislative process was an assignment she gave herself. She could feel the groundswell on any issue and know when to rush up to Capitol Hill and talk to her friends in Congress, or to anyone who had an influence on Congress. Behind her she had her troops; not only the power of the Children's Defense Fund, but the millions on whose behalf she spoke. Though her manner was often brisk and blunt she was nevertheless winning. Underneath the plain talk was her sincerity and her passionate concern for the millions of poor kids who needed love and protection. She wanted people in Congress to *feel* the need, to grip it emotionally and to act to save a child.

At any given moment, before Congress or at a conference or public meeting, she could express her outrage with a daunting command of facts:

"Every 13 seconds an American child is reported abused or neglected. Every 26 seconds an American child runs away from home. Every 59 seconds an American teenager has a baby."

She had developed her style of work in conjunction with the staff of the Children's Defense Fund. Like her, they were fully informed and alert. Every project called for a full discussion; the need to see it in its entirety then to break it down into what she called "manageable pieces for action." It would undergo close scrutiny to establish its immediate and long-term goals. Through all the discussions, Edelman was the vigilant overseer, meticulous about details and careful about realistic expectations.

The year 1988 held promise for a new national direction. Homelessness had created great public concern for social conditions and presidential elections would bring an end to the Reagan years. The time seemed favorable to introduce into Congress a new bill on child care. Edelman never forgot the 1971 Nixon veto of her child-care bill.

A coalition of more than 130 organizations, as well as the staffs of key members of Congress concerned with child care, helped CDF on preliminary work. After a year of detailed study, CDF wrote up a complex bill. It called for an expenditure in the first year of $2.5 billion to do three things: help families in need pay for child care, help states improve the quality and availability of child care, and establish federal standards for the funding of child-care facilities. Each state would adminster the funds, but day-care programs had to meet federal requirements.

Marian Wright Edelman, with CDF and the coalition of supporting organizations, succeeded in getting prominent members of Congress to introduce the Act for Better Child Care, known as ABC, in both the Senate and House of Representatives. Eventually 44 senators and 172 representatives cosponsored the bill.

No bill going through Congress has easy sailing, and this one faced typical problems. There were the complications of partisan disputes between Democrats and Republicans, some of whom were supporting an alternate bill introduced by Republican Senator Orrin Hatch of Utah. The Hatch bill, backed by conservative members of Congress, would cost less, but the funds would go to the states to administer, giving them greater flexibility to set standards of child care than the ABC bill. Edelman, from her experiences in Mississippi, knew the dangers of such a bill. A state might decide not to have equally good facilities for all children; it might be racist or neglect the poorest youngsters. Ultimately, Senator Hatch would move from his own bill and cosponsor the ABC bill.

The presidential year of 1988 seemed promising but Edelman was disappointed in Democratic Party candidate Michael Dukakis who showed no interest in the bill. Republican Party candidate George Bush announced his own plan for child care. The Bush Bill proposed a "children's tax credit," giving parents the choice of where to place their children, taking it out of the hands of the state.

Edelman saw the Bush proposal as inadequate but as a step in the right direction, for it was an admission that the federal government should assume responsibility for child care. The Bush proposal, she concluded, could be considered an addition to her bill, the ABC, rather than an alternative to it.

In the summer of 1988, the bill finally found its way out of committee and was reported to the full Senate in July and to the House in August. During its deliberations, Congress could feel the momentum set in motion by Edelman, the CDF, and the many mass organizations. Women in all parts of the country wrote to their congressional representatives, children sent drawings and letters, and CDF brought groups of children to Capitol Hill to press for the bill.

Children's Defense Fund rally at the White House to
support child-care legislation

While the fight was going on to have the child-care bill discussed, the Democrats and Republicans were planning huge political conventions for the presidential nominations. Skilled in public relations, CDF showered both conventions with leaflets and brochures on children's issues.

The November election of George Bush, who had shown interest in some kind of bill, nevertheless did not ease the battle for child care. It remained a tough fight but the hard work and perseverance of supporters promised a victory, and the bill passed the Senate and the House. Then, inexplicably, just before a conference was completed to work out the differences between the House and the Senate bills, the bill was pulled out.

Marian Edelman was shocked by the action. She was positive there was enough support to get the bill enacted. What happened? At the last minute, two early supporters of the bill unexpectedly withdrew their support. Key Democrats Tom Downey of New York and George Miller of California, both child advocates, said the bill, calling for $2.5 billion expenditure, did not have a chance of being signed by President Bush.

An enraged Marian Wright Edelman, in a personal attack on the two congressmen, sent them each a letter accusing them of acting "to sabotage groundbreaking child-care legislation all year for petty jurisdictional and power reasons." In addition, she claimed that "if child-care legislation is not enacted this year, the two of you will deserve the full blame for the tragic and unnecessary outcome."

She sent copies of the letter to members of Congress and to the newspapers. CDF resorted to the media and arranged for radio advertisements in Washington, urging congressional support for child-care legislation.

Edelman's clash with two liberal members of Congress led to shocked responses and a nasty war of words. Chairman Dan Rostenkowski of Illinois and ten other congressional members wrote to Edelman and defended the two representatives. "Tom Downey and George Miller are no enemies of

Marian Wright Edelman in 1990

children or child care; you know that as well as we do." Others called Edelman "petulant" and "inflexible." A few said Marian Wright Edelman had to learn to compromise. Republicans were strong in their condemnation. "She basically kicked her allies in the face," said Florida Representative Clay Shaw. Another spoke of her "holier-than-thou attitude."

Edelman was unconcerned about the loss of popularity and the harsh criticism. She did not mind being called a "bully," or "arrogant." Her only regret, she said, was that she "did not write the letter earlier."

Many came to her defense, among them Senator Hatch, who knew of her profound commitment to child welfare. "If she wasn't sincere, that would be another thing, but she's sincere as the day is long." On another occasion Hatch referred to Edelman "as one of the most formidable women in America today."

Members of Congress knew very well Marian Wright Edelman's work. They would rather not be recipients of her anger.

When the controversy subsided, Congress did pass a bill in 1990 for child care, allocating over $1 billion for the first year, as well as billions of dollars for expanded tax credits for low-income families. It was a fraction of what Edelman thought necessary and what her own Act for Better Child Care had requested. But it was a bill that recognized federal responsibility and provided significant new income for poor families through tax relief. As such, it was a victory for Marian Wright Edelman and the CDF.

CHAPTER FOURTEEN

A Leading Woman

WOMEN HAVE BECOME LEADERS IN THE NATION'S capital. The election in 1992 of 25 women to Congress and the appointment of women to cabinet and high administrative posts have given them a unique opportunity to change social policy. Marian Wright Edelman hopes they will make child care a legislative priority.

Heading the list of leading women is First Lady Hillary Rodham Clinton. An activist, she has established her credentials as a committed public advocate on behalf of child and health care, and has, for years, been an ardent supporter of the Children's Defense Fund. Donna Shalala, head of Health and Human Services, has been eager to meet the demands of the sick, the poor, and the jobless. A former chairperson and CDF board member, she is a close Edelman friend. Surgeon General Joycelen Elders took so many risks in making radical recommendations on behalf of children that President Clinton asked her to resign. Among other leading women are Attorney General Janet Reno, Environmental Protection Agency's Carol Browner, and Energy Secretary Hazel O'Leary.

Right on top, among the nation's leading women, is Marian Wright Edelman. Her impact on the Clinton administration has been profound, though she has chosen to be an independent and critical voice outside government. Insiders consider her the second most influential woman in Washington. Her prestige in the Clinton administration stems not only from her many years of public service but also from her friendship with Hillary Rodham Clinton that goes back almost 25 years.

Hillary Rodham was a student at Yale Law School in the spring of 1970 when she noticed an announcement on the bulletin board that former law school graduate Marian Wright Edelman was going to speak on campus. Marian and Hillary had met before at a Young Leaders Conference called by the League of Women Voters.

At the Yale Law School talk, Hillary was captivated by Edelman's knowledge and her passionate commitment to the welfare of children as well as by the force of her personality. Edelman, already arousing people to action, urged the students to use their law degrees to help change social policy.

Inspired by the talk, Hillary asked Edelman whether she could work for her during the summer. There were no funds to pay her, Marian explained. When Hillary was persistent and said she would raise the money some other way, Marian agreed.

Throughout that summer and subsequent years, Hillary's interest in children deepened. She began to observe children in nursery schools and to become informed about child development. She took additional courses to learn about children's legal status and family law. As her interest in children grew, she became a volunteer at the Yale Child Studies Center and continued course work on the legal protection of children. In 1973, the *Harvard Educational Review* published her article "Children under the Law," one of many she would write. She was also listed as a participant in CDF's study "Children Out of School in America."

Through Edelman, Hillary began to do research for the Carnegie Council on Children. Not only did she write legal papers for the council, but she also helped in research for the groundbreaking Kenneth Keniston book, *All Our Children.*

Upon graduation in 1973 from Yale Law School, Hillary became a staff attorney for the Children's Defense Fund in Cambridge. That lasted only a few months when she was tapped for a different job. But her commitment to children was permanent. Wherever she was, in whatever role, whether as wife of Arkansas Governor Bill Clinton or as the First Lady, she remained connected in one way or another to the Children's Defense Fund. In 1976, she served on the board of CDF and became chairperson of the board from 1986 to 1992, the year Bill Clinton was elected president.

The Bill Clinton presidency opened up an era of high hopes for child advocate Marian Wright Edelman and for all others committed to social legislation. Marian had a friend in the White House and to many observers, especially to those with an insider's view, she is considered part of the White House.

Hillary Rodham Clinton has been consistent and outspoken in her respect and affection for Marian Wright Edelman. At a talk at Spelman College in May of 1992, she said Marian had "helped give direction and shape to my life. . . . The world opened up to me and gave me a vision of what it ought to be because of the work of people like Marian."

At a CDF dinner that same month, the two women expressed their mutual admiration. Introducing Mrs. Clinton, Edelman remarked, "I know her in her role as a committed, extraordinarily persistent and thoughtful and balanced advocate and voice for children and families. . . . She knows the crucial need to nurture our families and to nurture our future Americans." The First Lady rejoined, "Thank you to my friend and mentor and leader of so many years now. Thank you, Marian, for your constancy and your persistence and your inspiration to so many of us in this room and around the world."

When Hillary Rodham Clinton spoke at a CDF dinner a year later, in November 1993, she made it clear that the CDF remained at the top of her agenda. She urged the 1,200 guests present to give their time and talents to the organization and help the nation's children. "There is a role for each of us as there is for every adult in this country to do better for our children," she said.

The Clinton administration, besieged by child advocates, has fulfilled some of its promise by signing into law measures long fought for. Among the gains in the year 1992–1993 was congressional approval of an increase in the Earned Income Tax Credit, which gives income support to working parents so they do not have to raise their children in poverty. The Childhood Hunger Prevention Act helps poor families deal with rising housing and food costs while meeting other basic expenses. A groundbreaking piece of legislation signed into law by President Clinton at a large ceremony was the Family and Medical Leave Act, which enables a working parent to take 12 weeks of unpaid leave to care for an ill member of the family. Another momentous presidential action has made available increased funds for the immunization of all children not covered by insurance and other programs. Such children were, in late 1994, eligible for free vaccines against childhood diseases, from their own physicians, clinics, or community and health centers.

Perhaps most encouraging to Marian Wright Edelman has been the Clinton administration's commitment to fully fund Head Start by 1999, "so that," according to CDF's *The State of America's Children Yearbook 1994*, "all eligible children have an opportunity to participate." After 30

Applauding President Clinton's signing of the Family and Medical Leave Act
in a Rose Garden ceremony. From left: First Lady Hillary Rodham Clinton,
Representative Richard Gephardt, Tipper Gore, George Yandle,
Marian Wright Edelman, Labor Secretary Robert Reich, and
Health and Human Services Secretary Donna Shalala

years of patient and persistent struggle, Edelman is reaping rewards in the Clinton presidency. For 1994, Congress appropriated an increase of $550 million for Head Start, making the total funding for the program $3.3 billion. Despite increased funding, only some 36 percent of eligible children were enrolled in Head Start in 1993. The programs, however, are being updated and expanded so that parents who work can feel secure that their children will be taken care of for the full workday.

Counteracting these gains have been reports showing a continued bleak picture. The *New York Times* headlined an article: POVERTY 1993: BIGGER, DEEPER, YOUNGER, GETTING WORSE. The article quoted Peter B. Edelman, who had become counselor to Donna Shalala's Department of Health and Human Services. "We lost our national will to do something about poverty," he said, referring to Presidents Reagan and Bush, who had shown "an unremitting lack of concern" about the problem.

In April 1994, another headline cried STUDY CONFIRMS SOME FEARS ON U.S. CHILDREN. Citing the results of a three-year study by the Carnegie Corporation of New York, the report said, "The plight of the nation's youngest and most vulnerable children is a result of many parents being overwhelmed by poverty, teenage pregnancy, divorce or work." It talked of "disintegrating families, persistent poverty, high levels of child abuse, inadequate health care and child care of such poor quality that it threatens youngsters' intellectual and emotional development."

Books, conferences, and reports have proliferated on the unhealthy conditions facing children and the ultimate effect on the country's future.

The gains in the Clinton presidency have benefited some sectors of the population but they have not touched the explosion of teen violence rocking cities and suburbs, nor teen pregnancy, nor AIDS and drugs. These painfully harmful excesses force new urgent demands, among them the need for jobs.

While Marian Wright Edelman has had high praise for President Clinton's increases in funding for some poor people's programs, she has said that the present dangers demand a fundamental change in priorities. She quoted the trillions of dollars the federal government spends in the global arms race. "Between 1968 and 1993," she pointed out, "the U.S. spent $29,000 per American to protect our children from perceived external enemies and far less to protect them from the real internal enemies of poverty, drugs, violence, and family breakdown." The present military budget, she has stated, is excessive given the end of the Cold War and the fact that the United States today is the sole Superpower. "Do we need a new aircraft carrier which will cost $5 billion in 1995 more than we need after-school and weekend and summer programs for children and youths?" she asked. Or "the $6 billion Sea Wolf submarine more than we need jobs to get parents off welfare?"

She is for strong national defense, she made it clear, but the Pentagon officials must also understand the needs of children and families "struggling for survival." Our political representatives should be pressured to make our country number one "in healthy educated children" rather than in the continued build up of "our current arsenal [that] already can destroy the world many times over."

She also carefully monitors proposals to "change welfare as we know it." She is vigilant that new initiatives do not push poor children and families deeper into poverty and that other changes do not destroy the safety net that makes it possible for poor children to survive.

Edelman can be tough and persevering, but she also takes pride in her organization's recent successes, among which are the 1990 child-care legislation, and the Education for All Handicapped Children Act. She hears the Clinton administration talk about "Putting Children First," and applauds its efforts. After 20 years of lobbying Congress, however, she sees that basic change in social policy will not come from inside the political process, but will come only from a mass national movement of people outraged by the conditions of children.

Though Edelman changed her work routine in the 1990s—preferring to work at home—she maintains complete involvement in CDF concerns and initiatives. She does so through weekly meetings in her office with her senior staff at CDF. They are heads of such departments as communications, programs and policy, finance, administration, and development. Once a month she meets with the entire CDF staff in the library. Here, the details of new projects are announced and discussed.

CHAPTER FIFTEEN

"Leave No Child Behind"

LIGHT STREAMS INTO MARIAN WRIGHT EDELMAN'S eighth floor corner office. The large bright space on the top floor of the Children's Defense Fund building on Capitol Hill is unpretentious. Windows cover two walls, another is lined with shelves of books and family photos, and on another hang large framed photos and posters, including images of Frederick Douglass, Mahatma Gandhi, Harriet Tubman, Albert Einstein, Albert Schweitzer, and W. E. B. DuBois. Prominently displayed between windows is a poster of the CDF logo, a child's drawing of a small boat on a large sea with the sailors' prayer. A long narrow desk is stacked with a neat pile of folders. A small round table is where she sits and talks to visitors.

Now in her mid-50s, she is a strong-looking, sturdy woman with large brown eyes and close-cropped hair framing an expressive face. In her 30 years' work defending and protecting millions of children, Marian Wright Edelman is recognized as the nation's most powerful child advocate.

A book fair in Bennettsville. Mrs. Amy Byers is seated to left of
Marian Wright Edelman. Standing from left: Peter Edelman,
Michael Cornwell, sons Joshua and Ezra, Marian's sister, Olive
Covington, and Olive's son-in-law and daughter, Dr. Edward
Cornwell and Dr. Maggie Cornwell

Always alive in her consciousness are her family and the community in
her hometown, Bennettsville, where her moral and spiritual strength were
nurtured. Writing about them and the moral precepts that drive her have
made her the author of a best-selling book, *The Measure of Our Success:
A Letter to My Children and Yours.* In it, she discusses her upbringing.
Then, in a section titled "Twenty-Five Lessons for Life," she talks to her
children and to all children examining in simple words the problems that
worry them. As a way of dealing with these problems, both political and
personal, she offers her own experience and that of others.

She has worried that she may have neglected her own family pursuing
the crowded schedule of what her son Jonah refers to as her "cause." But
she was always at home when needed. Breakfast with the family each
morning was never disrupted, and she would leave meetings to care for

a sick child. Her sons never felt out of touch with their mother, whom they were free to call any time of the day. As they grew up, they did feel the strict rules she imposed about viewing television or staying out late with friends.

Middle son Jonah, in a moving foreword to his mother's book, writes about his legacy: an ancestry of midwestern conservative Jews and southern black Baptists. Fortunately, he says, his parents, two people of different races and religions, forged their lives together in the days of the civil rights movement. That movement and its victories made it possible for him to accept himself as "the sheltered Bar Mitzvah boy who has struggled with his blackness."

To reinvigorate those ties of different races and religions, the Edelmans celebrated each son's coming-of-age in a ritual they called a "Baptist Bar Mitzvah" presided over by both a rabbi and a Baptist minister. On each

Marian Wright Edelman participating in Baptist Bar Mitzvah for son Ezra. At right, husband Peter; at left, son Joshua

occasion, Mrs. Edelman's brother, the Reverend Harry S. Wright, shared the ritual with the rabbi. During it, each member of the family spoke. Some 200 friends, relatives, and neighbors crowded into the Edelmans' large backyard in northwest Washington for the festive occasion.

To help her children understand the basics of the black religious experience, Mrs. Edelman took them twice a month to the Shiloh Baptist Church in Washington. There they also saw a segment of life different from their own middle-class interracial neighborhood. Never far from her mind are her worries about the resurging racial violence and her sons' safety.

Now fully grown and mindful of their upbringing, her sons have found their own directions. Joshua teaches at a private academy in Massachusetts; Jonah, a Rhodes Scholar, is in Oxford, England; and the youngest son, Ezra, is at Yale. They were raised to share their privileges with the less

Jonah, center, at his graduation from Yale in 1992. From left: his mother, brother Ezra, father, and brother Joshua

fortunate. Jonah points out that of his mother's "Twenty-Five Lessons for Life," three strike a response: (1) "Don't feel entitled to anything you don't sweat and struggle for. (2) Never give up. . . . Nothing worth having is ever achieved without a struggle. (3) Always remember that you are never alone. . . . There is nothing that you can ever say or do that can take away (my or) God's love."

Edelman knows very well that millions of parents cannot take advantage of the advice she offers in her book, that they must scrounge to meet simple basic necessities such as jobs, health care, food, and shelter. She points out that 63 nations worldwide provide family allowances to workers and their children but the United States is not one of those countries.

Her vow to make this country value and protect its children underlies the success of the Children's Defense Fund, which now has a yearly budget of over $15 million, a staff of 150, and its own building on Capitol Hill. Seven regional offices help carry out programs, and a research department and an aggressive communications office prepare a steady stream of publications that go to a large mailing list of educators, legislators, and public supporters.

CDF advocacy means not only working from an office in Washington and lobbying Congress; it also means educating the public, parents, and poor families about their rights and helping them find their own voices so that they can speak up in their communities. Essentially, CDF does what it was set up to do: it speaks for children and promotes investment in them so that they will not get sick, drop out of school, or suffer from a breakdown in family life.

Since 1990, CDF runs a yearly public luncheon to honor those who have beaten the odds. These children have made it against what is often called "the law of the streets" by resisting the lure of drugs, gangs, and violence or overcoming family situations. Consistently in the lives of such youngsters has been what Edelman refers to as "one caring lifeline out there," a supportive adult, teacher, or religious leader.

The Beat the Odds Luncheon is one way CDF personalizes its work. Children honored in 1994—Lonnie, Christina, Sean, Shaquita, LaToya, and Fernando—came to the platform, were introduced, and spoke frankly about their backgrounds and the problems they had to overcome. They are helped along with a cash award and commitments to their future.

CDF funding still comes from foundations, corporations, the public, and friends. Edelman welcomes support from corporate groups, remarking, "children need friends in all sectors of society, especially the corporate community. . . . We are thrilled that they are part of the growing national movement for children."

The wide net CDF throws over problems, its flexibility, strategies, and quick responses have made it a giant in the field of child advocacy. The staff of this non-profit, interracial organization—including lawyers, policy specialists, researchers, and community relations people—is emotionally committed and skilled.

But Marian Wright Edelman remains the driving force. The energy with which she urged a Senate subcommittee to investigate poverty in Mississippi in 1967 is the same high-powered energy with which she today pursues her concern for the country's millions of children. She never gives up. Strong, focused, and charismatic, her personality, like musical counterpoint, interlaces many voices. There is in her an accommodating and gracious presence, and at the same time a decisiveness—an alertness that can end in a cheerful laugh or a sharp remark. Her rapid-fire talk is more than a surge of words. It is a rush of ideas and thoughts tumbling after each other. Her mind makes connections to the past, the present, and to her vision of the future.

She is vigilant about any health plan that might be passed during the

Clinton administration—to be sure that it includes coverage for children. She and her staff carefully search each bill proposed and are ready to run up to Congress at a moment's notice to be sure no child is left behind. She is determined to make the nation understand that preventive investment in children must be central to United States policy.

Throughout, her sense of optimism does not waver. She continues to find ways of reclaiming the country's children where others might despair. "She is a fiercely eloquent spokesperson of children's rights . . . an important figure," said Dr. Howard Zinn.

Edelman also spreads the word and calls people to action through countless public-speaking engagements each year. Graduation exercises in particular, where she is often the guest speaker, appeal to her. They give her opportunities to stay in touch with young people, the nation's school graduates, to reach out to them and explain the importance of a moral commitment to others. She is in demand also for conferences, conventions, luncheons, and dinners as well as for television, newspaper, and magazine interviews. Wherever she talks, the basic concern is "child poverty in the United States must be ended." She explained to an interviewer that "our 1990s mission is to make it un-American for any child to be poor, unhealthy, uneducated, neglected, abused, a parent too soon, or deprived of hope."

Or she will want to know, "Where's the outrage to the young children who die from violence?" She will say, "It is evil to let children die when you have the capacity to save them." She will call on her religious background, "And I cannot believe for a moment that God's not going to punish a nation that has the capacity to save young lives and chooses not to."

Along the way she has become a board member of organizations, schools, and corporations. At the centennial celebration of Spelman College in 1981, Marian Wright Edelman was honored for, among other things,

Marian Wright Edelman in academic cap and gown addressing 1993 commencement ceremony at Southern Methodist University

Marian Wright Edelman walking with President Donald M. Stewart at a celebration of Spelman College Founders Day, 1981

being the first black woman to chair the board of trustees. In her talk at the symposium luncheon, she said, "You never run away and you never take anything for granted," as she urged her audience to become child advocates.

She has served on the boards of the March of Dimes, the Council on Foreign Relations, the National Alliance of Business, and many others.

High esteem and praise for her work have brought honorary degrees from Smith College, Swarthmore, Yale, the University of Pennsylvania, Rutgers University, and the list goes on. Awards and honors have added to her prestige from her first—the Merrill Scholarship for a year's study abroad in 1958–1959. She has become an Honorary Fellow of the University of Pennsylvania Law School. In 1979, she received multiple awards including the Presidential Citation of the American Public Health Association, Outstanding Leadership Award of the National Alliance of Black School Educators, and the Distinguished Service Award of the National Association of Black Women Attorneys. In 1985, she became a MacArthur Foundation Prize Fellow. In 1986, she delivered the W. E. B. DuBois lectures at Harvard. In 1988, she was the second person to win the Albert Schweitzer Humanitarian Award (the first winner was former President Jimmy Carter). She was the first African-American woman elected to the Yale University Corporation, and has served on the boards of many important civil rights organizations.

Her calendar for 1994 was full and typically included conferences, meetings, and another honor at the South Carolina Museum, where she was one of the "Black Women" honorees featured in the Brian Lanker book, *I Dream a World.*

How does she do it? How does she manage the hard work, the overflowing schedule? What about stress? Fatigue? Despair? Her personal philosophy helps her; she refers to herself as a "determined optimist."

Along with a sense of hope goes her long view of history and change: It takes time to build a movement and momentum. Even setbacks such as the Poor People's Campaign add to the whole struggle, and the whole struggle for her means, "Everything we hold dear depends on what we do for all our children today."

She also has personal resources and escapes. She calls the piano in her living room her "psychiatrist." Mornings she takes time to run her fingers over the keyboard. Often she plays sacred music, hymns, or she will recall a classical piece she learned in earlier years. Playing the piano is something she does for herself, to rest her mind and ease her into the day. Requiring quiet from time to time, she escapes to the meditation hut she had built in her garden where no telephone can reach her. She also takes long walks, reads, or works in her garden. When absolute quiet is essential to restore her sense of inner calm, she enters a religious retreat where silence prevails.

Stepping out from the past and comforting her are images of her childhood when family and community love offered a shield of protection and empowerment. Along with the nurturing strength came a responsibility. "I was taught," she said in a magazine article titled "First in Education" in the *American School Board Journal* in June 1991, "that the world had a lot of problems; that black people had an extra lot of problems, but that I was able and obligated to struggle and change them."

In her commitment to the poorest of the poor, she keeps the black communities visible, pointing out that they suffer disproportionately from society's ills. A January 1994 poll commissioned by CDF and undertaken in the black community confirmed Edelman's worst fears: "We have a black-child crisis worse than any since slavery."

Calling for a cease-fire in the war against children, Edelman has launched a new crusade to focus national attention on the gun violence that claims the life of a child in the United States every two hours.

Another initiative, the Black Community Crusade for Children, will take an active role within communities to reestablish the strong historic tradition of self-help and to build bridges between the generations and between the rich and the poor. In coalitions with other organizations, churches, and schools, the crusade's leaders call for health care, jobs, and job training and hope to reverse the trends within the black community, develop a youth leadership, and set the sights of the young on productive lives.

Tied in with the new campaign is the purchase of the Alex Haley farm by the Children's Defense Fund. Edelman sees the 127-acre Tennessee spread as a retreat, conference center, and as "a rigorous training school for a new breed of servant leaders." These leaders will then live and work in communities, offering children a link to the meaningful and loving adult that is so essential in their lives.

Edelman has also made clear her pride in African-American accomplishments. In an address to the Howard University class of 1990, she said, "Our black children need the rightful pride of a great people that produced Harriet Tubman and Sojourner Truth and Frederick Douglass from slavery, Benjamin Mays and Dr. King and Mrs. Hamer from segregation—people second to none in helping transform America from theoretical to a more living democracy."

Her voice and vision are everywhere. Audacious, imaginative, and determined, she continues to take on struggles that others have given up in despair. Her rallying cry has become a national slogan—LEAVE NO CHILD BEHIND!

Her greatest concern is "that I will not have lived as well or as pur-

Marian at a Columbus, Ohio, Head Start center in 1993
with Ohio Governor George Voinovich

posefully [as I should] or that I will not do what I was sent here to do." And because she feels she may fall short of her own high expectations, she pursues her work with almost religious zeal as if she has been divinely chosen for the mission. She has said, "I know why I have been put on this earth."

Others also know why she has been put on this earth. One of them is Mrs. Mae Bertha Cutler of the small town of Drew, Mississippi, with a population of 2,000. Mrs. Cutler told the *Los Angeles Times* in October 1990 that she had put eight of her 13 children in an all-white school in 1965. Mrs. Cutler herself had no formal education and grew up on a plantation picking cotton.

"We didn't have no food, no clothes, and they was shooting at us with the children all around the house!" she said.

Marian Wright had come to her rescue and successfully fought to keep the children in the white school.

The two women remained friends, and over the years Mrs. Cutler would always call on Marian for help. Couldn't she get help closer to home, she was asked.

"Why," she replied, "Marian Wright is one of the greatest women in America, don't you know that? Somebody has to do something for this generation coming on or else the United States is coming down. And who else but Marian Wright?"

O God Of All Children

O God of the Children of Somalia, Sarajevo, South
    Africa, and South Carolina,
Of Albania, Alabama, Bosnia, and Boston,
Of Cracow and Cairo, Chicago and Croatia,
Help us to love and respect and protect them all.

O God of black and brown and white and albino
    children and those all mixed together,
Of children who are rich and poor and in between,
Of children who speak English and Russian and
    Hmong and languages our ears cannot discern,
Help us to love and respect and protect them all.

O God of the child prodigy and child prostitute,
    of the child of rapture and the child of rape,
Of run or thrown away children who struggle
    every day without parent or place or friend or
    future,
Help us to love and respect and protect them all.

O God of children who can walk and talk and hear and
    see and sing and dance and jump and play

and of children who wish they could but can't,
Of children who are loved and unloved, wanted and
    unwanted,
Help us to love and respect and protect them all.

O God of beggar, beaten, abused, neglected, AIDS,
    drug, and hunger-ravaged children,
Of children who are emotionally and physically and
    mentally fragile, of children who rebel and
    ridicule, torment and taunt,
Help us to love and respect and protect them all.

O God of children of destiny and of despair, of war and
    of peace,
Of disfigured, diseased, and dying children,
Of children without hope and of children with hope
    to spare and to share,
Help us to love and respect and protect them all.

Marian Wright Edelman
THE STATE OF AMERICA'S CHILDREN 1992

ACKNOWLEDGMENTS

To a large extent personal interviews helped shape the contents of this book and give it direction. I would like to express my gratitude to Marian Wright Edelman for giving me her time and for providing details and images of many events. My deepest thanks to the Reverend Harry S. Wright for reaching back into the past to talk to me about growing up in the Wright family and for sharing family photos.

During my visit to Bennettsville, I was fortunate in meeting other family members and friends. I would like to thank Olive Wright Covington and Julian Wright for their personal warmth and for their memories of the early years. School friends, despite busy schedules, spoke about the old days. I would like to thank John Troy Henegan, Joan Blondell Dixon Johnakin, and teacher and adviser Tomasena Cupple Walker (Mrs. Floyd Walker). Romaine Covington Peguese, in a telephone interview, also reminisced about the school days and her friend Marian Wright. A. Ruth Thomas Peters was more than generous in helping with her remembrances of Bennettsville and Spelman College and in parting with memorabilia. I would also like to thank Editor/Publisher William Kinney, Jr., of the *Marlboro Herald Advocate* for recalling Bennettsville's past and for his memories of Mrs. Maggie Leola Bowen Wright.

Spelman College sisters Roslyn Pope and Virginia Powell Jeffries were generous in granting me telephone interviews and recalling college years. I would like to thank them and also Herschelle Sullivan Challenor.

I would also like to express my gratitude to the librarians and archivists in Atlanta, Georgia, who patiently searched for material for this book. In particular, I would like to thank Angela Hall, Research Assistant of Archives at Robert W. Woodruff Library, and Cynthia Lewis of the King Center Archives. At Spelman College, I am grateful for the kindness and patience of archivist Brenda Banks and Assistant Director of Alumnae Affairs Eloise M. Abernathy.

My gratitude to Professor Matthew Meade, who kindly explained the program of Operation Crossroads Africa during the summer of 1962 when he was also a participant.

I would like to give specific thanks to James Forman for a wide-ranging talk, and Dorothy Zellner for her encouragement and help in an early interview. Dr. Howard Zinn, in an informative phone discussion, gave me the benefit of his personal experiences at Spelman College and his memories of his student Marian Wright. I wish to thank him and Dr. Tom Levin, who, in personal interviews, also recalled Marian Wright and the heady days of the Head Start programs in Mississippi.

My thanks to Jon H. Goldstein for facilitating my research in Washington, D.C.

To the unfailingly helpful staff members of the Children's Defense Fund I would like to express my appreciation. Lauren Shapiro, Broadcast Specialist, made videotapes available. Paul Smith, Director of Research, and Renée Wessels, Director of Communications, did careful readings of the manuscript and offered helpful critical comments. Olive Wright Covington, Director, Children's Defense Fund, Marlboro County, also read the manuscript, and I would like to thank her for her insights. Above all, Stella Ogata, Media Associate, has my profound gratitude for her patience and courtesty in answering my many questions, for sharing photographs with me, and for helping me understand the broad scope of CDF activities.

Though in the past I have neglected to express my appreciation to the hardworking editors who oversaw my books, in this instance I would like to thank editor Virginia Duncan and assistant editor Andrea Schneeman for keeping a watchful eye on this manuscript.

PHOTOGRAPH ACKNOWLEDGMENTS

The photographs in this book were supplied courtesy of the Children's Defense Fund, Washington, D.C., except for the following:

Pages 58, 78, 88, 91, 96, and 123 courtesy of AP/Wide World Photos; page 138 courtesy of Bill Foreman Photography; pages 15, 20, and 128 courtesy of K. F. Hodges/LyBensons; page 134 (*top*) courtesy of H. S. Jackson, Southern Methodist University; page 51 courtesy of John Fitzgerald Kennedy Library (photo #AR7314-A); pages 59, 67, 68, 82, and 89 courtesy of the Library of Congress; page 29 courtesy of the Marlboro Training High School Senior Classbook; page 27 courtesy of A. Ruth Thomas Peters; page 43 courtesy of Roslyn Pope; page 17 courtesy of the Schomburg Center for Research in Black Culture; page 73 courtesy of the Schomburg Center for Research in Black Culture and the NAACP Legal Defense Fund; page 28 (*right*) courtesy of Beatrice Siegel; pages 31 and 32 courtesy of Spelman College; pages 38 and 39 courtesy of the Spelman College Classbook; page 134 (*bottom*) courtesy of the Spelman College Messenger; page 36 courtesy of the University of Geneva; pages 24, 26, 28 (*left*), and 47 courtesy of the Reverend Harry S. Wright; page 49 courtesy of Yale Law School.

SELECTED BIBLIOGRAPHY

To gather material for this book I have researched primary as well as supplementary sources: archives, newspapers, magazines, videocassettes, and film. Books about the period opened up the historical and cultural landscape and made it possible for me to trace the development of Marian Wright Edelman's ideas.

Essential are Edelman's own writings, among which is her book *Families in Peril: An Agenda for Social Change* (Cambridge: Harvard University Press, 1987). Here she describes conditions of those who have the least and urges a change in priorities. In *The Measure of Our Success: A Letter to My Children and Yours* (Boston: Beacon Press, 1992), an introspective Edelman offers thoughts on moral questions and suggests ways of living in today's world.

Her writings are also found in many journals. I call attention to *Yale Alumni Magazine* (February 1978), which carried her article "In Defense of Children's Rights," and *American Psychologist* (vol. 36, no. 2, February 1981), in which she writes "Who Is for Children?"

The State of America's Children Yearbook 1994 (Children's Defense Fund), with an introduction by Marian Wright Edelman, provides a current graphic picture of the country's needy children and the urgency for change.

Edelman's crusading fervor is captured in countless newspapers and magazines. The *Washington Post* (December 4, 1988) headlined Courtland Milloy's article, "A Firebrand Named Marian." In the *Los Angeles Times* (October 11, 1990), Geraldine Baum wrote about the "Children's Champion: Marian Wright Edelman Is a Feared Lobbyist and America's

Most Powerful Advocate for the Young." *Black Enterprise* magazine (May 1992) carried Matthew S. Scott's article on "The Great Defender," and the *Charlotte (North Carolina) Observer* (October 3, 1992) wrote about "Crusader for the Oppressed." A large spread in *Rolling Stone* magazine (December 10, 1992) told about "Marian Wright Edelman: On the Front Lines of the Battle to Save America's Children." Edelman herself wrote about "Kids First!" in *Mother Jones* magazine (April 4, 1994).

An in-depth study of Edelman's early years in Mississippi can be found in *Ebony* magazine (June 1966) in an article by journalist Ponchitta Pierce. She writes about "The Mission of Marian Wright: Young Woman Lawyer Forsakes Soft Life for Civil Rights Crusade in Mississippi."

Edelman publicizes her programs for children's rights in the many talks she gives at large gatherings such as the meeting of the National Press Club (Washington, D.C., April 14, 1992). She titled her talk "Vanishing Dreams: The Plight of America's Young Families." She can be seen and heard in interviews on videocassettes: "60 Minutes" (October 22, 1989), "World News Tonight with Peter Jennings" (March 29, 1991), "Larry King Live" (August 20, 1993), Charlie Rose (June 3, 1993), and Hollywood Women's Political Committee (May 27, 1993).

For general background material I recommend a few titles. Tony Dunbar's *Delta Time: A Journey through Mississippi* (New York: Pantheon Books, 1990) gives images of a poverty-stricken state and the rich culture of its poor people. Samuel G. Freedman's *Upon This Rock: The Miracles of a Black Church* (New York: HarperCollins, 1993) explores in detail the work of the pastor, the parishioners, and the community they strengthen. Allan Lomax's adventurous odyssey retrieves the music and survival gifts of an oppressed people in Mississippi in *The Land Where the Blues Began* (New York: Pantheon Books, 1993).

The sit-in movement and the growth of the Student Non-Violent Coordinating Committee have been subjects of scholarly studies and general literature. Among the many works I read while working on this book are Vincent D. Fort, "The Atlanta Sit-In Movement, 1960–1961: An Oral Study," a master's thesis in the Department of History of Atlanta University, 1980, and David Garrow's *Atlanta, Georgia, 1960–1961: Sit-Ins and Student Activism* (Brooklyn, New York: Carlson Publishing Co., 1989), and *The Sit-In Movement of 1960* by Martin Oppenheimer (Brooklyn, New York: Carlson Publishing Co., 1963, 1989). Among these worthwhile books are two by Howard Zinn: *SNCC: The New Abolitionists* (Boston: Beacon Press, 1964) and *The Southern Mystique* (New York: Alfred A. Knopf, 1964). James Forman's personal account, *The Making of Black Revolutionaries* (New York: Macmillan, 1972), reveals the critical struggles of the movement. Forman's book contains the full text of Bob Moses's letter from the Magnolia, Mississippi, jail.

Marian Wright's own words about people and events can be found in Henry Hampton and Steve Fayer's inclusive *Voices of Freedom: An Oral History of the Civil Rights Movement from the 1950s through the 1980s* (New York: Bantam Books, 1991).

Many books provide a detailed examination of specific aspects of the struggle. The brutal murder of young civil rights workers Chaney, Schwerner, and Goodman will be found in Seth Cagin and Phil Dray's descriptions of the harrowing events in *We Are Not Afraid* (New York: Bantam Books, 1991). The controversy around the Child Development Group of Mississippi is in Polly Greenberg's *The Devil Has Slippery Shoes* (New York: Macmillan, 1969). Sally Belfrage vividly describes the people and dramatic events of historic 1964 in Mississippi in her memoir *Freedom Summer* (New York: The Viking Press, 1965).

Visual history of the civil rights movement can be found in striking photographs of action and portraits in *The Movement: Documentary of a Struggle for Equality* (New York: Simon & Schuster, 1964), text by Lorraine Hansberry. Photographer Danny Lyons in *Memories of the Southern Civil Rights Movement* (Chapel Hill: University of North Carolina Press, 1992) provides pictures and commentary about SNCC's crucial struggles and its leaders.

The discussion of poverty in the United States in the 1960s and on can be found in many titles. Nick Kotz describes Senator Robert Kennedy's visit to the Delta and the Poor People's Campaign in a frank and compelling book, *Let Them Eat Promises: The Politics of Hunger in America* (Englewood Cliffs, New Jersey: Prentice-Hall, 1969). Revelations about the poor in the United States that startled the country are in Michael Harrington's book *The Other America: Poverty in the United States* (Baltimore: Penguin Books, 1963). All of Jonathan Kozol's books should be read, from his now classic and dramatic exploration of inner city education in *Death at an Early Age* (New York: Plume, Penguin Books, 1985) to the more recent *Savage Inequalities: Children in America's Schools* (New York: Crown, 1991). Finally, scholars Frances Fox Piven and Richard A. Cloward discuss political agendas in *Poor People's Movements: Why They Succeed and How They Fail* (New York: Pantheon Books, 1977).

INDEX